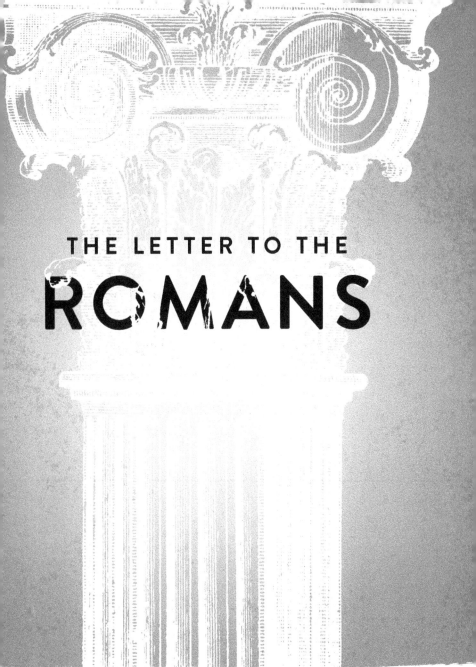

THE LETTER TO THE
ROMANS

THE BRIDGE BIBLE TRANSLATION

Connecting the Biblical to the Contemporary World

CONTENTS

1. Introduction: Faith in Christ puts people into a right
    relationship with God (1:1–17) 1

ROMANS CHAPTER 1 | page 1

    1.1   An overview of this letter: Paul indicates that God is calling all people
to faith in Christ (1:1-7).

        1.1.1   Paul shares his identity, calling, and purpose as the sender of this letter (1:1).

        1.1.2   Paul identifies the focus of this letter: to affirm the truth about Christ
and to call people of all nations—including the Romans—to live by
faith in Him (1:2-6).

        1.1.3   Paul identifies the people in Rome as the audience of this letter and
gives a general greeting and prayer for divine favor (1:7).

    1.2   The occasion of this letter: Paul is thankful that God has called the
Romans to faith in Christ and is eager to visit them to help deepen
their faith (1:8-15).

    1.3   The theme of this letter: Paul states clearly that those who have been
put into a right relationship with God will live by faith (1:16-17).

2. Human beings cannot put themselves into a right relationship
    with God, but God provides everyone a way to be right with
    Him by grace through faith in Jesus Christ (1:18–4:25) 5

    2.1   God's wrath is being revealed against all humanity because all miss the
mark and come short of God's standard (1:18–3:20).

        2.1.1   God's wrath is being revealed upon the non-religious people who do
not seek Him and miss the mark with God (1:18-32).

ROMANS CHAPTER 2 | page 7

    2.1.2   God's wrath is being revealed upon the hypocritical moralizers who like to judge others and miss the mark with God (2:1-16).

    2.1.3   God's wrath is being revealed upon the prideful and self-confident religious people who miss the mark with God (2:17–3:8)

ROMANS CHAPTER 3 | page 12

    2.1.4   Everyone misses the mark with God, and His wrath is being revealed upon the entire human race (3:9-20).

2.2   God puts people into a right relationship with Himself by grace through faith in Jesus Christ (3:21–4:25).

    2.2.1   Being put into a right relationship with God, being declared innocent of sin, and being saved from God's wrath all come to those who have faith in Jesus Christ (3:21-31).

ROMANS CHAPTER 4 | page 18

    2.2.2   Being justified and put into a right relationship with God happens through faith alone, and faith has always been God's way (4:1-25).

3.   **As a result of being put into a right relationship with God through faith in Christ, there is a new power of God working in the lives of the faithful for their salvation (5:1–8:39) . . . 23**

ROMANS CHAPTER 5 | page 23

3.1   The new power of God working in people's lives brings the hope of final and ultimate salvation (5:1-21).

    3.1.1   Those who are right with God through faith experience hope in their lives (5:1-11).

    3.1.2   Those who are right with God through faith experience the reign of God's grace and His new life through Christ (5:12-21).

ROMANS CHAPTER 6 | page 29

3.2   The new power of God working in people's lives frees them from bondage to sin (6:1-23).

    3.2.1   Through faith in Christ, human beings are dead to the power of their sinful nature and alive to God's power working in them (6:1-14).

    3.2.2   Through faith in Christ, human beings are freed from sin's power and enslaved to God's spiritual power, which leads to right living (6:15-23).

ROMANS CHAPTER 7 | page 33

3.3   The new power of God working in people's lives frees them from the
      bondage of trying to earn our way to God (7:1-25).

      3.3.1   Human beings are released from the non– life-giving standards of
              trying to keep the Old Covenant Law and joined to God's New
              Covenant of grace through Christ (7:1-6).

      3.3.2   Human beings recognize the problem of indwelling sin within them
              through the help of the Old Covenant Law (7:7-25).

ROMANS CHAPTER 8 | page 39

3.4   The new power of God working in peoples' lives gives them the
      assurance of eternal life in the Spirit (8:1-30).

      3.4.1   The Spirit fills people with God's new kind of life (8:1-13).

      3.4.2   The Spirit helps people recognize that they have been fully adopted
              into God's family, and to realize that they will inherit all He has for
              them (8:14-17).

      3.4.3   The Spirit helps people to have perspective on their present suffering
              and to realize the reality of future joy and glory with God (8:18-30).

3.5   The new power of God working in peoples' lives can be celebrated
      because nothing can ever separate those who have faith in Christ from
      the love of God (8:31-39).

      3.5.1   Those who have faith in Christ have five certainties about how God
              works in their lives (8:28b).

      3.5.2   Those who have faith in Christ can know the five stages through which
              God achieves their salvation (8:29-30).

      3.5.3   Those who have faith in Christ can ponder five questions that help
              settle the matter of salvation in their hearts (8:31-37).

      3.5.4   Those who have faith in Christ cannot be separated from the love of
              God (8:38-39).

4.   God has been working through the past, present, and future to
      fulfill His promise and form a global community of people who
      belong to Him and reflect His character (9:1–11:36) 48

ROMANS CHAPTER 9 | page 48

4.1   The issue: Given the tension between God's promises to Israel in the
      Old Covenant and their current rejection of God's New Covenant
      revealed in Christ, does that mean that God cannot be trusted to keep
      His promises? (9:1-5)

4.2   In the past, God worked through the Old Covenant nation of Israel to
      form a spiritual people who would belong to Him and be prepared to
      receive Christ (9:6-29).

4.2.1   God called and formed a new, spiritual Israel who genuinely belonged to Him within the Old Covenant people of Israel (9:6-13).

4.2.2   God is not unfair or unjust in choosing who belongs to Him. God is free to do whatever He desires with His creatures and creation (9:14-23).

4.2.3   God foretold that He would call a new, spiritual people to belong to Him. They are formed not by national, personal, racial, social, or any other factors but by His calling and grace (9:24-29).

4.3   In the present, Old Covenant Israel is missing out on what God is doing through Christ (9:30–10:21).

4.3.1   Since Old Covenant Israel has stumbled by failing to have faith in Christ, and since the Gentiles have not stumbled and believe, it may appear to be an upside-down world (9:30-33).

ROMANS CHAPTER 10 | page 56

4.3.2   Many people from Old Covenant Israel have failed to recognize God's New Covenant work in Christ (10:1-13).

4.3.3   The path to salvation is through faith, but many people from Old Covenant Israel choose not to believe in Christ (10:5-13).

4.3.4   People from Old Covenant Israel have heard God's message through Christ and are responsible for their rejection of Him (10:14-21).

ROMANS CHAPTER 11 | page 60

4.4   Even though the people of Old Covenant Israel are missing out on God's work in the present, God is still at work forming a global, spiritual community of people who belong to Him (11:1-10).

4.5   Even though the Gentiles make up the majority of God's people in the present, just imagine what an amazing future is available to the people of Old Covenant Israel if they turn to Christ (11:11-32).

4.5.1   God is accomplishing a larger purpose through Old Covenant Israel's rejection (11:11-16).

4.5.2   The pride of the New Covenant Gentiles could cause them to become lifeless, spiritual deadwood (11:17-24).

4.5.3   In God's sight, there is no difference between Jew or Gentile. All must come to Him the same way—through faith in Christ (11:25-32).

4.6   Praise God for how He has been working in the past, present, and future to make His salvation available to everyone (11:33-36)!

5. As a result of being brought into a right relationship with God through faith in Christ, God's people experience transformed relationships and transformed perspectives in every aspect of life (12:1–15:13). 67

ROMANS CHAPTER 12 | page 67

5.1 God's people experience a transformed relationship with God by continually consecrating their bodies to Him and by renewing their minds through His truth (12:1-2).

5.2 God's people experience a transformed relationship within themselves when they realize they are all part of the same body of Christ with other believers (12:3-8).

5.3 God's people experience a transformed relationship with one another by loving others as if they are family (12:9-16).

5.4 God's people experience a transformed relationship with their enemies not by retaliating against them but by serving them with sincere love (12:17-21).

ROMANS CHAPTER 13 | page 71

5.5 God's people experience a transformed relationship with governing authorities in society by submitting to and respecting their authority (13:1-7).

5.6 God's people experience a transformed relationship toward God's moral law by embodying the love of Christ, which fulfills the Law (13:8-10).

5.7 God's people experience a transformed relationship toward the end of time by realizing that God is working in His people now to develop in them the fullness of life that is yet to come (13:11-14).

ROMANS CHAPTER 14 | page 74

5.8 God's people experience a transformed relationship toward those who have different religious perspectives and practices by realizing that what unites them as part of God's family is stronger and more important than their differences (14:1–15:13).

5.8.1 Do not condemn and pass judgment on fellow members in your family of faith (14:1-12).

5.8.2 Do not act in such a way that will cause your brother or sisters in Christ to stumble spiritually (14:13-23).

ROMANS CHAPTER 15 | page 79

    5.8.3   Follow the example of Christ and put other people first (15:1-6).

    5.8.4   Christ fulfilling God's promise brings God's divine favor to all who have faith. As a result, treat each person of faith as though they are dearly loved family members who belong to God (15:7-13).

6.   Conclusion: God is at work through Paul's ministry (15:14–16:27). 81

    6.1   Paul reflects on all that Christ has done in and through him and on his future ministry plans (15:14-21).

    6.2   Paul shares his immediate travel plans to visit the people of Rome on his way to Spain (15:22-29).

    6.3   Paul requests prayer from the Romans (15:30-33).

ROMANS CHAPTER 16 | page 84

    6.4   Paul sends personal greetings to a variety of people in Rome (16:1-16).

    6.4.1   Paul commends one of his ministry colleagues (16:1-2).

    6.4.2   Paul gives his personal greetings (16:3-15).

    6.4.3   Paul encourages the Romans to welcome each other and sends greetings from other churches (16:16).

    6.5   Paul shares a final message and praises God for His plan of salvation through Christ (16:17-27).

    6.5.1   Paul's warning: Avoid divisive persons (16:17-20).

    6.5.2   Paul's friends send their greetings (16:21-24).

    6.5.3   Praise God for His salvation through Christ (16:25-27).

—

ROMANS

—

1. Introduction: Faith in Christ puts people into a right relationship with God (1:1–17).

1.1 An overview of this letter: Paul indicates that God is calling all people to faith in Christ (1:1-7).

CHAPTER 1

1.1.1 Paul shares his identity, calling, and purpose as the sender of this letter (1:1).

¹This letter comes to you from Paul, one who has freely chosen to be a slave of Christ Jesus. God has called me to serve Him by being an apostle, one of His twelve authorized representatives who have been entrusted with His message. The purpose and focus of God's calling on my life has been clear. I have been set apart and permanently appointed to share the gospel of God—to proclaim what He has said and what He has done with others. I did not invent the gospel; it comes from God.

1.1.2 Paul identifies the focus of this letter: to affirm the truth about Christ and to call people of all nations—including the Romans—to live by faith in Him (1:2-6).

[2]Right here, at the start of this letter, let me affirm the truth about the gospel of God. God's gospel—His good news—fulfills what He promised long ago through the prophets. It fulfills what was written by His prophets in the Holy Scripture of the Old Covenant [Old Testament]. The gospel of God forms a New Covenant with His created world through the person and work of Christ. [3]The substance of the gospel is God's son Jesus Christ, who has worked among us in two distinct stages. The first stage focused on His earthly life. Jesus was born into the ancestral family line of David, fulfilling the human existence the Messiah was expected to have. [4]The second stage focused on His divine essence. Through the Spirit of holiness, Jesus was shown to be the Son of God with divine power when He was raised from dead. Fully human and fully divine–Jesus Christ is our Lord.

[5]In sharing the gospel of God, I am called to focus on the people of all nations. Through Christ, God has given me the unique privilege of being a special authority to tell all the non-Jewish people [Gentiles] what God has done for them. My aim in sharing the gospel is always the same: to lead and call people of all nations to the obedience of faith. In leading and calling people to faith, my goal is to help everyone see the all-surpassing worth and value of God in both who He is and what He has done. [6]And my calling to focus on all nations includes you—all of you who are in Rome. You are within the universal scope of God's message, and He has called you to belong to Jesus Christ.

1.1.3 Paul identifies the people in Rome as the audience of this letter and gives a general greeting and prayer for divine favor (1:7).

[7]I am writing this letter to all of you in Rome. None of you are excluded from belonging to God based on your nationality, ethnicity, religious background, or the like. You all are loved by God and called to be His people who reflect His divine character and qualities.

To all of you in Rome: May God our Father and the Lord Jesus Christ give you His unmerited favor and the peace of well-being that comes from knowing Him.

1.2 The occasion of this letter: Paul is thankful that God has called the Romans to faith in Christ and is eager to visit them to help deepen their faith (1:8-15).

[8]I want to begin by saying that I continually thank my God through Jesus Christ for all of you. Why? Because you have a reputation for a strong faith in Christ, which is being talked about all over the world. [9]God—whom I serve with all my spirit and soul—is my witness and knows how often I mention you [10]in my daily prayers. I also plead with God that, if it pleases Him, He will make a way for me to come to Rome and finally visit you in person. [11]I long to see you so that I can share with you the spiritual insights God has given me; they will help you grow even stronger in the Lord. [12]But I do not want to visit you only to give but also to receive. For when I am able to visit, I know we will be mutually encouraged by each other's faith.

[13]I hope you know, my brothers and sisters in Christ, that I have planned to visit you many times. However, thus far, I have been prevented from doing so. Yet, when I do visit, I am confident that we will see the spiritual fruit of people turning to the Lord, just as I have been seeing throughout the Gentile world. [14]Like a person who has been given money to invest and is indebted to that person to use it wisely, I have been entrusted with sharing the gospel with the Gentile world. It does not matter who others think you are—a civilized, high-cultured Greek; an uncivilized barbarian; or an educated or uneducated person—I have an obligation to share the gospel with you. [15]As result of my calling, this passion that drives me, and this joyful debt I feel, I am eager to communicate the gospel—God's good news—with all of you who live in Rome.

1.3 The theme of this letter: Paul states clearly that those who have been put into a right relationship with God will live by faith (1:16-17).

[16]I am not ashamed to communicate God's good news with you, and let me tell you two reasons why. First, it is the power of God that makes salvation—the final deliverance from sin, evil, death, and separation from God—universally available to everyone who believes. It is first good news to the Jews, since God has been preparing them throughout the Old Covenant's [Old Testament's] history to receive the Christ. Then, it is good news to remainder of the Gentile world which has now also received God's invitation to salvation.

[17]The second reason: In the gospel, the righteousness of God is revealed. And what does the righteousness of God mean and look like? It means that in the good news about Christ, we see how God (who is just, pure, and morally complete) puts human beings (who are unjust, impure, and morally incomplete) into a right standing with Himself. This reality of being put into a right relationship with God only happens by His grace and through His divine intervention in our lives. And how does God make it possible for us to be right with Him? Only through faith in Christ from beginning to end. It is just like what is written in the Old Covenant Scripture of Habakkuk 2:4: "The person who is made right with God through faith shall live."

2. Human beings cannot put themselves into a right
    relationship with God, but God provides everyone a
    way to be right with Him by grace through faith in
    Jesus Christ (1:18–4:25).

2.1 God's wrath is being revealed against all humanity because all miss the mark and come short of God's standard (1:18–3:20).

> *2.1.1 God's wrath is being revealed upon the non-religious people who do not seek Him and miss the mark with God (1:18-32).*

[18]While the gospel reveals the righteousness of God, let me be clear on why it is necessary. We need God to put us into a right standing with Himself because His holy wrath is being revealed—in the past, present, and future—from heaven against human sinfulness. It is being revealed against all the godless attitudes of those who show no reverence for God. And God's holy wrath is not an emotional outburst or overreaction; it is a necessary response from a Divine Being who is morally pure and perfect. God's holy wrath is also being revealed against all the wicked and immoral behaviors of people, which destroy human relationships. These people are experiencing God's holy wrath because their wickedness and immorality are hindering the truth and restraining it from affecting their lives.

[19]What is more, these people know better, for they are not without some knowledge of God. God allows His holy wrath to touch them because He has made some aspects of His existence crystal clear. It is plain and obvious, yet these people have rejected any knowledge of God. [20]Since the creation of the world, one can look around and see and know that God created it. By looking at everything He made, all people can understand God's invisible qualities—His eternal power and divine nature. Yet, people hinder and restrain the truth from affecting their lives. The result: people have no valid excuse for failing to know God and live for Him. They have earned God's wrath by rejecting Him.

²¹Even when they knew and recognized God, they still did not honor and value His worth, nor did they give Him thanks for all He has done. Instead, their thinking became futile and their foolish hearts were darkened. ²²Although they thought they were creative, smart, innovative, and wise, they became fools. ²³Instead of honoring and valuing the all-surpassing worth of the immortal God, they exchanged it for "gods" they created and thought they could control. They crafted their version of "god" into idols with images made to look like mortal human beings, birds, reptiles, and other animals—things they thought they could understand, manipulate, and control.

²⁴Therefore, God abandoned the people who hindered the truth from affecting their lives; He gave them over to the sinful desires of their hearts. As a result, they degraded and dishonored their bodies in sexual impurity with one another. ²⁵They exchanged the truth about God for their own lies. They honored, valued, and served their own creations instead of the Creator who made them—the Creator who is forever worthy of being praised and will always be so!

²⁶For this reason, God abandoned these people who hinder and suppress His truth from affecting their lives. He gave them over to their shameful lusts and allowed them to pursue their unnatural passions. Their women exchanged natural sexual relations with men for unnatural ones. ²⁷Likewise, men also gave up natural sexual relations with women and were consumed with lust for one another. Men committed unnatural sexual acts with men. Just like anyone given over to their sinful desires, they received in themselves—mind, body, and soul—the due penalty for their error.

²⁸Since these people did not approve of God's truth and thought it foolish to acknowledge God and live for Him, God gave them over to their unapproved, corrupted minds and allowed them to pursue their own depraved thinking, letting them do things that should not be done. ²⁹And do not think for a second that sin is limited to just one aspect of our lives, or that it only affects our affections (creating idols, our own version of god), our passions (desiring unnatural sexual relations), or our thinking (depraving our mind). Sin is a universal and widespread human condition affecting everyone in some way.

These people who have suppressed God's truth from affecting their lives have become filled with every kind of wickedness, evil, greed, and all kinds of sinful behavior. They are filled with sins that affect and destroy relationships—sins such as envy, which causes them to have ill will and bad intentions toward others because of some real or perceived advantage; murder; strife, which causes them to never say anything good about one another; deception; and malicious behaviors, words, and acts that harm others. They are gossips who spread rumors and create divides between people, [30]slanderers who want to destroy the reputation of others, and people who speak against or hate God. They are insolent people who attack others—sometimes violently—because they think they are better than others. They are arrogant people who exaggerate their own worth or think too highly of themselves, which leads to boasting and bragging about themselves. They are people who invent new ways of doing evil and who disobey and dishonor their parents when they get in the way. [31]They refuse to learn and understand, refuse to keep their promises, refuse to show love and kindness, and refuse to show empathy or compassion for others. [32]Although they know God is holy—knowing His justice requires that those who do these sinful things deserve death and divine punishment—they not only continue to do these evil and unholy behaviors, but, even worse, they encourage and approve of others who practice these sinful acts.

> 2.1.2 God's wrath is being revealed upon the hypocritical moralizers who like to judge others and miss the mark with God (2:1-16).

CHAPTER 2

GOD'S JUDGMENT IS INESCAPABLE (2:1-4).

[1]You may be prone to condemn these "immoral" people because they suppress the truth, do wrong, and approve of unholy, immoral behavior. But do you realize that you are just as bad? You do wrong but act like you do not. And even though you do wrong, you strongly condemn others for their wrong or immoral actions. You are bunch of moralizing hypocrites! Do you realize that when you pass judgment on others, you are condemning yourselves as well? And do you

wonder why that is? It is because you are essentially doing the same things as those you condemn! It may be of a different type or form of sinful behavior, but the essence of what you are doing—suppressing God's truth from affecting your life—is the essentially the same. ²But make no mistake, you do not fool God. He knows your hypocrisy. And we know that God is just and right when He judges, for His judgment against people's sinful acts is based on truth and justice.

³Did you think that by judging others for their sinful acts you would somehow earn credit with God so that He would overlook what you do? Did you think you could escape God or avoid His judgment for your similar sinful acts? ⁴Or maybe you assume that because God is rich in His loving-kindness, His ability to endure without irrationally responding, and His willingness to be patient you somehow have a blank slate to do whatever you want without any consequences? Do you not realize that the reason God shows His loving-kindness to you is to lead you to repent, which means to turn away from your sin—mind, body, and soul—and turn your entire life's orientation towards following Him?

GOD'S JUDGMENT IS COMPLETELY JUST AND MORALLY RIGHT (2:5-11).

⁵But the simple reality is that God misses nothing. Because of your stubbornness and your unrepentant hearts, refusing to turn from your morally and spiritually deviant ways, you are merely stockpiling fuel that will be added to the fire of God's wrath against you. For the day of God's wrath is coming, when the fullness of His righteous judgment will be unleashed on all unrighteousness for everyone to see.

⁶God will repay each person according to what they have done. ⁷To those who, by continuing to do good, show they are seeking God's glory by continuing to do good, live for what is honorable, and realize they are spiritual beings who will live forever, God will give a new kind of life that eternally endures. ⁸But for those who are self-seeking, who refuse to follow the truth of God's teachings, and whose lives are guided by sinful and immoral behavior, they will experience the justice of God's holy wrath and fury.

⁹It does not matter who you are. There will be troublesome suffering and great distress for every human being who habitually does what is wrong in God's sight—first for the Jew (since God has worked throughout history to prepare them to receive His truth), then also for the Gentile (for they know better and are also without excuse). ¹⁰However, God will give glory, honor, and peace to everyone who habitually does what is right in God's sight—first for the Jew (since God has worked throughout history to prepare them to live and reflect His truth), then also for the Gentiles (for they can know God as well). ¹¹It does not matter what your religious heritage, nationality, or ethnic background is or how morally right you think you are, because God does not show any favoritism to anyone. He judges all by the same divine standard.

GOD'S JUDGMENT IS IMPARTIAL (2:12-16).

¹²Regardless of who you are, everyone will be judged fairly and justly by what they know about God. However, do not think that is a loophole to escape His judgment. Do not think you can plead ignorance before God; we all know better and hinder God's truth from affecting our lives. Even those who have sinned without any specific knowledge of God's moral standards contained in the Mosaic Law (the first five books of the Old Covenant [Old Testament] Scriptures), including the Gentiles who do not have the Mosaic Law, will also perish. Because based on the general knowledge they did possess about God, they still sinned against Him. Likewise, all who have sinned with some knowledge of God's Old Covenant Law (such as the Jewish people) will be judged by what they did know of God's moral standards. ¹³For it is not those who hear God's teachings or know something about them that are made right in God's sight. Instead, it is those who apply God's teachings and put them into practice who will be declared innocent and be in a right standing before God.

¹⁴For example, when the Gentiles (who do not have direct knowledge of God's moral standards written in the Mosaic Law) do by natural instinct what the God's standards require, they demonstrate that some aspect of God's moral law resides within them as human beings. And even though they have never heard of and do not know God's

standards for life written in the Mosaic Law of the Old Covenant, [15]their actions show that God's standards—His requirements and expectations for human character—are written on their hearts and woven into the fabric of all humanity. Their inner beings confirm whether they are doing right or wrong, and their consciences and thoughts either accuse them or defend them. [16]So, to all you moralizing people who like to judge others, the gospel I share is clear: the day is coming when God will judge everyone's secret thoughts and entire life through Christ Jesus, no matter who you are.

> *2.1.3 God's wrath is being revealed upon the prideful and self-confident religious people who miss the mark with God (2:17–3:8).*

EVEN RELIGIOUS PEOPLE MISS THE MARK AND COME SHORT OF GOD'S GLORY (2:17-24).

[17]You may be prone to think that both the non-religious and the moralizing hypocrites deserve God's wrath, but do you realize that even you—the religious people—are just as bad? You do not and cannot fully practice what you preach. You base your false sense of spiritual security and overconfidence on religious privileges that you enjoy. And you have a lot of religious advantages they do not have:

1) You call yourself a "Jew," meaning you identify yourself as belonging to God's chosen people identified from the beginning of the scriptures of the Old Covenant.
2) You have been given the moral laws revealed in the Old Covenant and rest your hope in keeping them.
3) You are proud of and celebrate your special "chosen" status with God.
4) [18]You know what God's will is because you know the Old Covenant's teachings.
5) You are able to discern right and wrong because you have been instructed in the moral laws of the Old Covenant.
6) [19]You are confident that you have the religious life all figured out—and are good with God—because you serve as a guide to the blind, a light to those who are in darkness.

7) ²⁰You feel assured with God because you have a well-developed and robust understanding of the moral laws revealed in the Old Covenant—His revealed knowledge and truth.

8) You serve as instructors of people you consider ignorant or irreligious fools, and teachers of those who are like infants in their religious knowledge and growth.

²¹However, even though you have all these things, you have a major problem! Just because you are teaching others, that does not mean you are practicing what preach. If you can teach others so well, why do you not teach yourselves better? For example, you who preach against stealing, do you ever steal? ²²You who speak out against adultery, are you having your own illicit affairs? You who claim to abhor idols (gods we have created, imagined, or shaped), do you use materials taken from pagan temples when it is to your advantage to use them, even though it is against your tradition and you claim to hate idolatry?

²³You are so proud and boast about knowing God's moral laws, but you dishonor God and harm His reputation in the world by breaking those laws. ²⁴We have seen religious people dishonor God's name and reputation in the past, and we have seen it have drastic consequences on non-religious. Isaiah 52:5 highlights how God's people caused Him to be mocked where, in essence, it says, "The non-Jewish, non-religious Gentiles blaspheme God's name because of you religious people."

OUTWARD RELIGIOUS PRACTICES AND CEREMONIES CANNOT MAKE ONE RIGHT WITH GOD (2:25-29).

²⁵And if your possession and knowledge of God's moral laws does not excuse you from God's judgement, do you think the religious tradition of being circumcised does any better—that an outward symbol of belonging to God helps you escape His judgment? Circumcision has value only if you observe and keep every law of the Old Covenant. However, if you do not observe and keep every part of God's moral law, then you are no different than a non-religious person who has never been circumcised. You become just like those uncircumcised Gentiles you consider so ungodly and do not like.

²⁶On the other hand, what if these uncircumcised Gentiles that you look down upon observe and keep God's moral laws better than you do? If that happened, would God not recognize them as His people? Would He not look at them as though they are circumcised, since their lives were more of a sign that they belong to Him than yours are? ²⁷In fact, in this scenario, these uncircumcised Gentiles that have kept God's moral standards would condemn you Jews—the ones who have been circumcised and who were originally given God's moral laws. They would condemn you because you do not actually observe or keep all the moral standards of the Old Covenant.

²⁸Are you seeing who the real people who belong to God are? A person is not a Jew (meaning someone who belongs to God) by outside appearances or associations alone. Having been outwardly and physically circumcised is not enough. ²⁹Instead, a person is a Jew who is one inwardly. True circumcision—the kind that matters to God—is a matter of the heart, an inward circumcision that marks the core drive of one's being. This heart circumcision does not happen by obeying every outward detail of God's moral law; it happens by the inner workings of God's Spirit inside the human soul. And the person whose heart has been changed inwardly by the Spirit seeks praise not from other people, but from God.

CHAPTER 3

RELIGIOUS PEOPLE MAY LIKE TO THINK THEIR HISTORY, HERITAGE, RITUALS, STANDARDS, OR PRACTICES MAKE THEM SPECIAL OR EARN THEM FAVOR WITH GOD, BUT THEY, TOO, MISS THE MARK AND COME SHORT OF GOD'S GLORY (3:1-8).

¹Right about now, some objections to what I have said may be coming to mind. So, let us address them. The first objection: Does this teaching about the gospel undermine God's covenant promise to the Jewish people—those who were given the Old Covenant—when it comes to being a part of God's family? Do they have any religious benefits that the Gentiles do not share? Is there any value to their outward circumcision?

²Since everyone is judged by the same standard before God, it may seem there is no religious benefit for those of Jewish heritage. But that is not the case! We must separate how God will ultimately judge a person from points in our religious history that we can be thankful for. Those with a Jewish heritage can be thankful for several religious privileges they enjoy. Jews of the Old Covenant were entrusted with God's moral teachings and guidance for life, and He worked through them to prepare the way for His full revelation of Himself to the world.

³A second objection that may be coming to mind: Does this teaching imply that God is unfaithful to His promises? Since God was working through the Jewish people and some of them were not faithful to God in the past, does that mean God cannot be trusted to keep His promises and to finish the work that He starts?

⁴No way! Absolutely not! Even if every person in the world was a liar, God would still be true. People cannot diminish God's faithfulness. He keeps His promises and continues to work through fallen people when they turn back to following Him. Even after David sinned with Bathsheba, he attested to God's character, truth, and faithfulness in Psalm 51:4, where he wrote, "God, you will be proven right when you speak, and you will win your case when the judgement is made."

⁵The third objection that may be coming to mind: Does this teaching mean God is unjust? If our unfaithfulness and injustice provide God with a better way of showing His perfect moral character and justice—as it did through the crucifixion of Christ—then is God being unfair when He punishes human beings for their sin? (I cannot believe I am writing these words. It is an embarrassing thought, but somebody is likely thinking it).

⁶The answer: no way! Absolutely not! If God were not entirely fair and completely just, how could He possibly judge the world?

⁷The fourth objection that may be coming to mind: Does this teaching mean we should violate God's will and sin even more in order to better promote God's glory? Some might think, "Well, if my lies and

sinful ways serve to make God's truth stand out more clearly, then why am I still being condemned as a sinner? Does my sinfulness not help God receive more glory?"

⁸This line of thinking—as some like to slanderously claim that we teach—is absurd. Why not go all the way and say, "Let us totally disregard God's standards and God's will and do more evil that good many come of it!" People who think or say such things deserve the just condemnation they will receive.

> 2.1.4 *Everyone misses the mark with God, and His wrath is being revealed upon the entire human race (3:9-20).*

⁹Well then, what should we conclude? Do we Jews have any spiritual benefit that makes us more right with God than the Gentiles? When it comes to God's wrath, are we of Jewish background any better off than they are? Nope! Not at all. For we have already made the spiritual, criminal case before God that both Jews and Gentiles alike are all under the power and influence of sin. All are guilty of deviating from God's ways. All are addicted to sin and held captive by it.

¹⁰The Scriptures of the Old Covenant make it clear that everyone is under the power of sin. Everyone is guilty of deviating from God's way and violating His moral standard. As a result, they will not escape God's holy wrath against them and their sin. You can see this truth in these seven passages I am about to share, which are connected like links on a chain to demonstrate the reality that we all have sinned and will not escape God's holy wrath.

The first two passages show how we all are ungodly and not right with God in some way. Ecclesiastes 7:20 says, in essence, "There is no one who is just, right, and morally complete before God; not even one. ¹¹There is no one who understands enough; there is no one seeking God completely." ¹²In Psalm 14:1-3, it is written that, "All have turned away from God. Together, they have all become worthless. Not a one of them can do enough good or be right enough to ever meet God's standard, not even one."

[13]In the next five passages, we see how pervasive sin is and how it taints and corrupts every part of our human existence. In Psalm 5:9, it is written that, "Their throats are like old, open graves that give off a foul stench. Their tongues are filled with lies." Psalm 140:3 says, "Every word they speak is like the deadly poison of a viper." [14]Psalm 10:7 declares, "Their mouths are full of cursing and bitterness." [15]In Isaiah 59:7, it is written that, "Their feet are swift to resort to violence and shed blood. [16]Ruin and misery are scattered all along their path, [17]and they know nothing about the way of peace." [18]And Psalm 36:1 says, "There is no reverential fear of God before their eyes."

[19]Now, it would be easy to assume that these Scriptures from the Old Covenant are only talking about the Gentiles' sinfulness and their need for a right standing before God—about how they deserve His wrath. But that is not the case. These truths apply to everyone, including the Jews! Everything in the Mosaic Law of the Old Covenant applies to those to whom God's moral law was given.

But what is the purpose of this larger discussion about human sinfulness? The purpose is to reveal that, when we all are individually on trial before God and giving an account of our lives, every mouth will be silenced in our attempts to make excuses, self-justifications, and rationalizations. We must recognize that none of us has an adequate self-defense for our sinful guilt before God. We must realize that everyone—the entire world, with no exclusions—will be held accountable to God.

[20]Therefore, no one will be declared innocent in God's sight, for none of us can fully live according to His moral standard and will. Whether Greek or Jew, it does not matter who you are—things done in obedience to the Mosaic Law of the Old Covenant can never make you right with God. You can never do enough good or religious things to earn His favor. You can never transform your character enough to be acceptable before a 100 percent holy and just God. Instead, God's moral law makes us all aware that we have sinned. Through God's moral law, we all become conscious of our sin—how we deviate from God's ways and violate His moral standard. Through God's moral laws, we become fully knowledgeable about our sin, and we recognize that we all stand guilty before God with no possibility of defense.

2.2 God puts people into a right relationship with Himself by grace through faith in Jesus Christ (3:21–4:25).

2.2.1 *Being put into a right relationship with God, being declared innocent of sin, and being saved from God's wrath all come to those who have faith in Jesus Christ (3:21-31).*

THROUGH THEIR FAITH IN CHRIST, GOD PUTS PEOPLE INTO A RIGHT RELATIONSHIP WITH HIMSELF (3:21-23).

²¹But now, I have the most amazing news ever! God has made known to us a new way to be right with Him—one that does not depend on our efforts to earn God's favor (which we cannot do anyway). In this new way, God is the One who acts and does the work to make us right with Him. And this new way of being right with God fulfills what He promised in the Old Covenant Law of Moses and the Prophets. ²²In this new way, in this New Covenant between God and human beings, God brings everyone who believes into a right relationship with Him through their faith in Jesus Christ. And everyone needs it! Because when we are standing before God, there is no difference between one's race, nationality, or religious background. ²³For all have sinned—it is part of everyone's cumulative past throughout human history. We all fall short daily of God's glory. We are made in God's likeness and created to reflect His holy character in every way, yet we come short of God's created purpose for our lives every day.

THROUGH THEIR FAITH IN CHRIST, GOD DECLARES PEOPLE NOT GUILTY OF THEIR SIN AND LOOKS AT THEM AS THOUGH THEY HAVE NEVER DONE ANYTHING WRONG (3:24).

²⁴But God, by His grace, and under no requirement or compulsion to do so, freely makes us right in His sight through faith in Christ. By His free grace and unmerited favor, all who have faith in Christ are justified before God. Through Christ, God finds no evidence for a guilty verdict against those who believe; He looks at those who have faith as though we have never done anything wrong. How is that possible? God did this through Christ Jesus, who had paid the price to free us from the guilty verdict and just penalty we deserve for our sins.

THROUGH THEIR FAITH IN CHRIST, GOD FULFILLS HIS MORAL STANDARD AND HIS JUSTICE BY ACCEPTING JESUS' SACRIFICE ON BEHALF OF THOSE WHO BELIEVE (3:25-26).

[25]How did God do it? Well, a holy, just, and morally perfect God could not leave human rebellion against His ways unpunished, nor violation against His moral standard unaccounted for. But God, in His grace, presented Jesus Christ as the sacrifice for our sins and rebellion against His standard. Through His sacrifice and the shedding of His blood, Christ took the punishment we deserve. When we receive Christ by faith, His blood sacrifice, poured out on our behalf, covers over our sin and makes us right with God. In doing this, God also demonstrates His justice for those who broke God's moral law before Christ's sacrifice, because He had been holding back His full punishment against their sins until the time of Christ. [26]God also presented Christ as our sacrifice to demonstrate His justice against sin in the present time, for God is both just in His holy character—having to punish violations against His moral law—and the One who justifies those who have faith in Jesus Christ.

THROUGH FAITH IN CHRIST, GOD PROVIDES EVERYONE WITH THE SAME OPPORTUNITY TO HAVE A RIGHT RELATIONSHIP WITH HIM (3:27-31).

[27]From this amazing teaching, I can imagine three questions that might come to mind. Let me address each of them. Question 1: Do we Jews have any accomplishments to brag or boast about that set us above the Gentiles and make us more acceptable to God than they are? No. In Christ, there is nothing that sets us above another person, race, or nationality. There is no achievement of ours for us to boast in. Such boasting is excluded and unnecessary, because our salvation is achieved by what God did for us through Jesus Christ.

As a follow-up to the same question, you may be asking: What principle or rule is this based on? Does this truth come from the Old Covenant Law of Moses, which emphasizes that our relationship with God is based on fully obeying God's law? No, it is based on the principle of faith in Jesus Christ, which is our source and motivation for following God's teaching. None of us are any better than anyone else, since we all stand before God as sinners, and each of us can only made right with God through faith in Christ. [28]For we fully affirm that a

person is justified—declared not guilty and put into a right relationship with God—only through faith. It does not happen by observing
and doing what the Old Covenant Law of Moses commands.

²⁹Question 2: Is God the God of the Jews only? Or is He also the God
of the Gentiles? Yes, He is the God of the Gentiles too. ³⁰There is only
one God, and He does not discriminate. God will bring everyone—
regardless if they are a circumcised Jew or an uncircumcised Gentile—
to a right relationship with Himself through faith.

³¹Question 3: By focusing on faith for salvation, does that mean the
Mosaic Law in the Old Covenant scriptures is useless and unimport-
ant? No way! Not by any means! Instead, we uphold the Old Covenant
Law of Moses as God's righteous standard for holiness. We affirm that
God's moral laws and requirements from the Old Covenant have now
been completely fulfilled in and through Jesus Christ.

> 2.2.2 Being justified and put into a right relationship with God
> happens through faith alone, and faith has always been
> God's way (4:1-25).

CHAPTER 4

ABRAHAM DID NOT RELY ON ANY OF HIS OWN ACTIONS OR EFFORTS BUT WAS JUSTIFIED BY FAITH (4:1-5).

¹From this amazing teaching about God bringing us to right relationship with Himself through faith, I can almost hear another question
you may have: How does all of this relate to Abraham? God's promise
to His people—and to us who are Jews ethnically—began with our
spiritual forefather Abraham. We Jews are his physical descendants.
We are prone to look at Abraham's obedience as the foundation of
God's promises. So how does this New Covenant teaching of being
made right with God through faith relate to Abraham? Is there any
continuity between Abraham and this New Covenant teaching of
salvation by grace through faith? What did Abraham teach on this
matter?

²We often look at Abraham as a model of faithfulness to God's moral law—a model of how to rightly live with God. Our thoughts are often jumbled in terms of how his obedience, faith, and relationship to God's moral law all come together. We are prone to make the mistake of overemphasizing Abraham's obedience—as though his obedience led to God's promise of salvation, or as though Abraham earned or caused God to give him His lasting promise. So let us state the obvious: If God's favor could ever be earned through obedient acts, then Abraham would have something to boast about, right? However, that is not God's way, and our focus must be on what God has done, not Abraham.

From God's perspective, no one can be justified by works. Abraham, like everyone else, has no right to boast before God about what he has done. Before God, even Abraham cannot make himself holy; he cannot do enough to make himself right with God. Instead, just like everyone else, Abraham was brought to a right relationship with God through faith. ³The Scriptures of the Old Covenant clearly make this point about Abraham's faith in Genesis 15:6, where it says, "Abraham believed God, and because of his faith, God has gifted a credit to Abraham's account, giving him something he did not have before: a right standing before God."

⁴We are used to earning and working for what we have. When people work, their wages and paychecks are not given to them as a gift. Instead, their wages have been earned through their efforts. ⁵However, that is not how things work in God's economy. God gives His grace and unmerited favor freely and without any constraint. There is no action, deed, or level of obedience that will obligate God to give anything. Therefore, God gives people a gift that we cannot earn through their efforts—a credit of His grace that goes into their accounts. He gives people this gift not because they have earned it through their actions or obedience, but because they have placed their faith in God, the One who declares the ungodly not guilty of their sin and restores them to a right relationship with Him.

DAVID DID NOT RELY ON ANY OF HIS OWN ACTIONS OR EFFORTS BUT WAS JUSTIFIED BY FAITH (4:6-8).

[6]This concept of being brought to a right relationship with God through faith is not just limited to Abraham. David teaches the same thing in the beginning of Psalm 32. There, David describes the divine favor and joy known by those who are declared right with God, the divine favor they have been given apart from any work they have done. Psalm 32:1-2 says, [7]"Filled with divine joy are those whose transgressions—whose disobedience to God's moral law—are forgiven, whose sins are covered over as though they were never there. [8]Filled with divine joy are those whose record of sin the Lord will not count against them."

ABRAHAM WAS JUSTIFIED BY FAITH, NOT BY TRUSTING IN HIS RELIGIOUS HERITAGE, CEREMONY, OR PRACTICES (4:9-12).

[9]In talking about how Abraham was made right with God through faith, I can almost hear another set of questions coming to your mind: Who has access to this divine joy you just mentioned? Does it belong only to the Jews, who are Abraham's physical descendants because they have been circumcised, or is it also for the Gentiles who are not physical descendants of Abraham because they have not been circumcised?

We have been saying that God accepted Abraham's faith, and that He gifted to Abraham's account a credit of something he did not have before—a right standing with God. [10]But how did Abraham receive this credit from God? Did he receive it after he was obedient to be physically circumcised or before? The answer: It was not after but before he was circumcised. [11]Abraham received circumcision after he already had faith in God. Some of the Jewish scholars even estimate that Abraham's circumcision came 29 years after he believed. So, circumcision was an outward sign of an inward reality. It was a seal symbolizing the right standing Abraham had with God through faith before he was ever circumcised. God's purpose in this was not only to make Abraham the spiritual father of all who been circumcised but also of all those of a different background who have not been circumcised. In this way, Abraham is the spiritual father of all who believe. For all who believe receive a gift in their account—a credit which God gives freely to all of those who are in His family of faith—that brings them to a right relationship with God.

[12]Yes, Abraham is the spiritual father of the uncircumcised who believe. But Abraham is also the spiritual father of those who have been circumcised—that is, if they follow in his footsteps by placing their faith and trust in God. I hope you see that what matters here is not one's physical, religious, or racial heritage, nor the outward, physical act or ceremony of circumcision. What matters is the spiritual dynamic and whether one trusts in God. For everyone who trusts in God has Abraham as their spiritual forefather.

THE PROMISE OF GOD'S SALVATION IS GRANTED AND REALIZED THROUGH FAITH (4:13-25).

Faith, not obedience to moral law, secures the promise of salvation (4:13-15).

[13]Also, it is important to realize that when God promised in Genesis that the entire world would be blessed through Abraham and his descendants, He made that promise not because Abraham had earned it by obeying the laws of the Old Covenant. Instead, God promised it because Abraham believed; Abraham was brought into a right relationship with God through faith. [14]For if God's promises only belong to those who have the Scriptures of the Old Covenant Law and obey them, then faith means nothing. God's promises would be worthless because they would totally depend on human obedience. [15]You may be thinking that sounds fair—the idea that you get what you deserve based on your obedience—so why would that be a problem? It is a problem because it is impossible for human beings to obey God's moral law completely. And those who have the Scriptures of the Old Covenant know that God unleashes His holy wrath on those who do not fully keep His moral standards.

Now, since the Old Covenant Law reveals that God's holy wrath rests upon those who cannot keep His standards, you may be thinking that we would be better off without these scriptures containing God's moral law. But that is not the case! If there were no laws of the Old Covenant, then there would be no direct awareness of what it means to disobey Gods' moral standards. We would never realize that we cannot fully keep God's law. Without the laws of the Old Covenant, we might not recognize our need for God's grace and unmerited favor.

Faith secures the promise of God's salvation for everyone who believes, and it comes as a gift of God's grace (4:16-17).

[16]Since human beings cannot earn God's favor or obey His moral law perfectly, that is why God's promise of salvation is based on faith. It is received by faith so that God's promise of salvation can be given freely as a gift out of His grace. And through faith, God's promise is guaranteed to all of Abraham's spiritual offspring. Thankfully, God's promise of salvation is not limited only to those who share a Jewish heritage and follow the Jewish religious customs of the Old Covenant. Instead, God's promise is for everyone who has faith in God—just like Abraham did. In this way, Abraham is the spiritual forefather of everyone who believes. [17]It is just as the Scriptures teach us in Genesis 17:5: "I have made you the father of many nations." God has fulfilled His promise to Abraham just as He said He would. This promise is still true in the presence of the God in whom Abraham believed—the God who gives life to the dead and calls things that did not exist into existence.

Faith is based on trusting in God's promise of salvation (4:18-22).

[18]When all hope seemed lost, Abraham continued to believe and put his hope in what God had said—that he would become the spiritual father of a vast multitude of people in many nations. For God had said to him, "Your descendants shall be as vast and countless as the stars." [19]Even when faced with the hopeless physical evidence of his own hundred-year-old body (which seemed almost as good as dead) and that his wife's womb was well past normal child-bearing years, Abraham's faith in God never weakened. [20]He never wavered in believing God's promise of salvation. Instead, his faith only grew stronger as he continued to affirm that God is the ultimate value and worth in life. [21]Abraham was fully convinced that God had the power to do what He had promised. [22]His faith in God was the basis of his hope. With a heart full of faith, God "gifted a credit to Abraham's account, giving him something he did not have before: a right standing with God."

Faith is not just for those in the past, but it is the means through which everyone can have a right relationship with God (4:23-25).

23Given that you likely have questions about how God's truth related to our spiritual forefather Abraham, and how God's plan of salvation is consistent with God's promises in the Old Covenant, I have shared a lot about Abraham. But let us not lose sight of what these truths mean to us as followers of Christ. What God said about Abraham—that "because of his faith, God has gifted a credit to his account, giving him something he did not have before: a right standing before God"—was not written for him alone. 24What was written belongs to all of us and is for our benefit too! Because of our faith in the One who raised Jesus Christ our Lord from the dead, God will give us the gift of a credit to our accounts as well, which is the credit of being brought into a right relationship with God and having a right standing with Him. 25Because of our sins, Jesus was delivered over to death and was raised to life in order to put us into a right legal standing with God, a legal standing where God declares us not guilty of any sin or wrongdoing and looks at us though we have never done anything wrong.

3. **As a result of being put into a right relationship with God through faith in Christ, there is a new power of God working in the lives of the faithful for their salvation (5:1–8:39).**

    3.1 **The new power of God working in people's lives brings the hope of final and ultimate salvation (5:1-21).**

    3.1.1 Those who are right with God through faith experience hope in their lives (5:1-11).

CHAPTER 5

THOSE WHO ARE RIGHT WITH GOD THROUGH FAITH HAVE HOPE AND PEACE WITH GOD (5:1-5).

1So far in this letter, we have talked extensively about how we have been justified by God through faith. We have talked about our new legal status with God where, by faith, we are declared not guilty of any sin, disobedience, or wrongdoing—where we are treated as if we have never done anything wrong.

Now, let us transition toward two new topics:

1) how we can be certain and assured of our justification, and
2) how God's power works in us in our continuing struggle against sin, and how it works against efforts at self-justification when we try to keep God's moral law.

Let us start by talking about the certainty and assurance we can have because of our new legal status with God.

Since we have been justified through faith, we have received and experience several proofs that help us be certain of our new legal status in Christ. The first proof of our justification is this: We have peace with God, a peace that not only gives us a general sense of well-being in life but also of living in a state of harmony with God. We have this peace with God only through our Lord Jesus Christ.

²The second proof of our justification: Through Christ and faith in Him, we have gained access into a constant state of grace, in which we now live. And we can be confident and rejoice in the hope not only of experiencing the restoration of glory that was lost because of sin but also in looking forward to sharing in the experience of God's glory throughout eternity.

³The third result of our justification: Not only will we share in God's glorious future throughout eternity, but we can continue to be confident and rejoice because we know God is working in and through our present sufferings. Why? Because we know God uses suffering to build perseverance in our lives; ⁴and by building perseverance, it leads to a more developed and proven character; and by building a stronger character in Christ within us, it leads us to be stronger and more confident in the hope of our salvation and the recreation of all things.

THOSE WHO ARE RIGHT WITH GOD THROUGH FAITH HAVE HOPE BECAUSE GOD HAS BROUGHT THEM INTO A RIGHT RELATIONSHIP WITH HIMSELF THROUGH CHRIST (5:5-8).

[5]This hope we have will not disappoint us. How can we be so sure? First, this hope will not disappoint us because we have both subjective (what we feel on the inside) and objective (what we can verify on the outside) evidence of God's love for us in Christ. Our subjective, internal evidence is this: God's love for us has been poured into our hearts and fills them through the Holy Spirit, who is God's gift to us. [6]Our objective, external evidence is this: At just the right time in human history, even though we were sinners who had turned away from God and we were utterly powerless and helpless in our ability to be right with God, Christ died for us.

[7]Do you grasp how amazing His love is? Very rarely would someone be willing to die to save the life of a person they respect. Although, perhaps someone might be willing to die for a good person they cherish and care for. [8]But God took it a step further. God demonstrates His own love for us in this: While we were still sinners who hated and rebelled against Him, Christ died to make it possible for us to have a right relationship with God.

THOSE WHO ARE RIGHT WITH GOD THROUGH FAITH HAVE HOPE BECAUSE OF WHAT GOD HAS DONE FOR THEM IN CHRIST (5:9-11).

[9]Second, this hope will not disappoint us because God has done for us the work we could not do ourselves; He has done this work through Christ. Since we have been justified and made right in God's sight by the blood of Christ (with His blood covering over our sins), how much more certain is it that we will be saved from God's wrath on Judgment Day through Him! God has already done the hardest work for us through Christ. Compared to the difficulty of what He did for us on the cross, saving us from His judgment will be extremely easy.

[10]We used to be God's enemies, but He reconciled us and brought us into a right relationship with Himself through the death of His Son. If God was willing to reconcile us when we were still His enemies, even through the death of His Son, then surely now that we are His

reconciled friends, we can be confident He will save us from eternal death and His wrath through Christ's resurrected life!

[11]In short, we can be certain that our hope in Christ will not disappoint us. We can confidently rejoice in this hope because of what God has done for us through our Lord Jesus Christ. It is through faith in Him that we have now received a reconciled relationship with God.

> 3.1.2   *Those who are right with God through faith experience the reign of God's grace and His new life through Christ (5:12-21).*

THE CONSEQUENCE: SIN AND UNIVERSAL DEATH CAME INTO THE WORLD THROUGH THE ACTIONS AND REBELLION OF ADAM AGAINST GOD (5:12).

[12]In order to gain a greater appreciation for the power of God—the power that makes us certain of our hope and salvation—let us now compare the effects of Adam's actions and Christ's work on our lives. Let us start with Adam.

- Sin came into the world through the actions of Adam.
- And Adam's sin brought a spiritual death.
- And this spiritual death spread to all people and is universal among all human beings.
- As a result, all people sinned in and with Adam.

THE COMPREHENSIVE NATURE: SIN AND DEATH WERE ACTIVE IN THE WORLD EVEN BEFORE ANY HUMAN BEINGS HAD ANY KNOWLEDGE OF GOD'S MOSAIC LAW (5:13-14).

[13]Before moving on in this comparison between Adam and Christ, let me take a brief detour to say a bit more about the universal nature of sin and death:

Even before the Mosaic Law of the Old Covenant [Old Testament] was given, you can be certain that sin was in the world. However, sin was not charged against anyone's account before God the same way back then. For the people did not yet know the Old Covenant Law of Moses. [14]However, sin's universal effect of death still affected humanity. From the time of Adam to the time of Moses, death reigned over the entire human race. It even reigned over those people who had not sinned by directly breaking or disobeying a command from God, as Adam did. But Adam—the one who disobeyed God and brought sin to all humanity—is a type, a symbolic representation, of the One who was yet to come, the One who would forever change the human predicament through His obedience to God.

THE CONTRAST: ADAM INTRODUCED SIN INTO THE WORLD BUT CHRIST IS GOD'S GIFT OF GRACE TO ALL HUMANITY (5:15-17).

[15]Let me be crystal clear: There is a tremendous difference between the effect of Adam's sin and the effect of God's gift of grace. For if many have experienced spiritual death and separation from God through Adam's disobedience, then how much greater has God's grace and His gift of forgiveness overflowed to many through another man, Jesus Christ?

[16]There is also a tremendous difference in the result of Adam's sin and the result of God's gift of grace. The result of Adam's sin caused humanity to be guilty and condemned at God's final judgment. But the result of God's free gift of grace delivers the undeserved verdict of being declared not guilty before Him, to be looked at by God as though we have never done anything wrong, even though we are guilty of many sins.

[17]But if death reigned over all humanity because of Adam's sin, how much greater will be the outcome through another man, Jesus Christ! All who have received God's abundant grace and the free gift of being made right with Him will reign in a new kind of life through Christ.

THE COMPARISON: THE RESULT OF ADAM'S SIN IS DEATH BUT THE GIFT OF GOD IS A NEW KIND OF LIFE THROUGH CHRIST (5:18-19).

[18]Now, to pick up my train of thought from the beginning of this section where I started comparing Adam and Christ:

Just as Adams' one deliberate, sinful act of disobedience against God resulted in condemnation for the entire human race, so also Jesus Christ's one good act of complete obedience to God resulted in our justification. For those who trust in Christ, they are not only declared not guilty of sin and free from it but they also now have a new kind of life and relationship with God. [19]Just as through the disobedience of one person (Adam) the many were inaugurated into a spiritual state and disposition of sinfulness, so also through the obedience of the One Man (Jesus) the many will be inaugurated into a spiritual status of being in a right relationship with God.

THE CONCLUSION: GOD'S GRACE REVEALED THROUGH CHRIST REIGNS THROUGHOUT ALL ETERNITY (5:20-21).

[20]Now you may be thinking that by talking about Adam and Christ I have left out Israel. What about all the things God did for them? One thing God did through them was to establish His standard with humanity by giving them His moral law in the Old Covenant. And the Mosaic Law was given so that people might see they cannot fully keep God's moral standards and realize they are indeed sinners before a perfect, morally complete, and holy God. And it was intended that where the knowledge and awareness of sin increased, it would increase people's appreciation and desire for God's grace and His unmerited, divine favor even more.

[21]So, do you see the overall picture here in comparing Adam's sin and God's grace to us through Christ? Humanity's power and ways are insufficient to save us. But by trusting in God's power, we can be certain in the hope of our ultimate and complete salvation. For just as sin has ruled over human beings and brought death and separation from God to us all, so now God's grace rules in those who have faith in Him, which brings us to a right standing with God and leads us to reign in the kind of life that eternally endures through Jesus Christ our Lord.

3.2 The new power of God working in people's lives frees them from bondage to sin (6:1-23).

3.2.1 Through faith in Christ, human beings are dead to the power of their sinful nature and alive to God's power working in them (6:1-14).

CHAPTER 6

THOSE WHO ARE UNITED WITH CHRIST THROUGH FAITH PARTICIPATE IN HIS DEATH AND RESURRECTION (6:1-5).

[1]Since we followers in Christ have been brought into a right relationship with God and are assured that our eternal life with Him is secure, what does all of this mean for our present lives? Since our eternity is secure, does that mean we do not need to worry about our morality and ethics in the present? If our sinning causes grace to increase, should we not sin more so that God's grace might also increase?

[2]No way! Absolutely not. For us who have faith in Christ, a decisive shift in the state of our being has occurred. We have died to sin, and we no longer live under its dominating power. Since we are in a state of death to sin, how can we go on living in it any longer? [3]Do you not realize that when we all were converted and brought into a union with Christ Jesus through our baptism, that we were also immersed into His death—immersed into a status where the power of sin could no longer affect us?

[4]Upon our conversion to Christ, we are identified with and become participants in what He has done for us. We have been buried with Christ through our baptism—becoming dead to the power of sin over our lives. And just as Christ was raised from the dead by the glorious power of the Father, we, too—right now—share in and experience a new kind of life that is like Christ's.

THOSE WHO HAVE FAITH IN CHRIST ARE NO LONGER ENSLAVED TO SIN BECAUSE THEY ARE UNITED TO HIS DEATH (6:5-7).

[5]Since we have become fused together with Christ through His death, we have died to the power and effects of sin. But we are not only fused

together with Christ's death but also His resurrection. As a result, we will certainly also be united with His resurrection and share in a new life that looks just like His. ⁶We can also be certain of the result of dying with Christ. For we know that our old self—our entire being before we were converted—was crucified with Christ in order that sin might lose its power over our lives. The effect of this is that we are no longer be enslaved by the power of sin. ⁷For when our lives were fused together with Christ through faith, we died with Christ. At that time, we were unshackled from the power of sin. We are no longer slaves to it, and we are free to live in the power of a new kind of life.

THOSE WHO HAVE FAITH IN CHRIST EXPERIENCE THE NEW POWER OF HIS LIFE LIVING IN THEM BECAUSE THEY ARE UNITED TO HIS RESURRECTION (6:8-10).

⁸And we can be certain of the result of being raised with Christ too. For we know that if we have died with Christ, then we have faith in two realities: 1) that we will also be physically resurrected with Him in the future, and 2) that we enjoy now the first fruits of living a new kind of life that will endure eternally with Him. ⁹We know that since Christ was raised from the dead, He can no longer be in a state where He is affected by sin. Death no longer has any power over Him. ¹⁰When Christ died, He died once to forever break the power of sin over humanity. And now, He lives in the fullness of a new kind of life, one that is perfectly empowered to carry out God's will and purpose.

THOSE WHO ARE NO LONGER ENSLAVED TO SIN BECAUSE OF CHRIST'S DEATH HAVE THE NEW POWER OF LIFE IN THEM BECAUSE OF HIS RESURRECTION (6:11-14).

¹¹Since God has broken the power of sin over us through Christ, you should be motivated to live freely and morally in this new kind of life. In order to live this way, one thing you can do is to constantly see yourself as one who is dead to the power of sin but alive to the power of God, the One who empowers you to live out this new kind of godly life. ¹²To live this new kind of life free from sin, it is imperative that you take the following actions: You should not let sin have power over your life and rule over your mortal bodies. You should not give in to your sinful desires. ¹³Do not let any part of your bodily existence—whether a skill, capacity, or ability—become an instrument of evil

that serves sin. Instead, completely give yourselves to God because you have been out brought from spiritual death and into new life. Be sure to use every part of your body as an instrument to do what is right and to do what reflects your right relationship with God. [14]For sin shall no longer be you master. You no longer live under the old regime of the Old Covenant [Old Testament] Law of Moses, where you were a slave to the power of sin. Instead, you now live under the new regime of God's New Covenant of grace, where you are free from sin's captivity and rule over your life.

> 3.2.2 Through faith in Christ, human beings are freed from
>   sin's power and enslaved to God's spiritual power, which
>   leads to right living (6:15-23).

[15]We just talked about how God's grace and unmerited favor give us a new freedom into a new life. We talked about how this new spiritual power working in us frees us from the burden of trying to earn our way to God by trying to perfectly keep the Mosaic Law of the Old Covenant. But I can almost hear someone thinking this question: Since God's grace has set us free from the burden of the Old Covenant Law, does that mean we can go on sinning—doing whatever we want—without it affecting our life with God? No way! Not by any means!

[16]You see, in God's universe, there are two different spiritual and religious powers at work. There is the "sinful power of this present age," which is dominated and ruled by the influence of sin, death, and the Devil; this power does not follow God's ways. Then there is the "godly power of a new age that has come," which is dominated and ruled by the influence of God, which eradicates sin, defeats death, and destroys the Devil; this power is devoted to following God's ways. And thanks to Jesus Christ's crucifixion, resurrection, and ascension, this godly power of God's new age has already come, and it is working among us right now!

Do you not realize that you belong to—and are actually serving as a slave to—one of these spiritual powers at work in the world? It does not matter if you consciously signed up or not. By virtue of being a human being, you are not just a member belonging to one of these spiritual dynamics, but you are actually a slave that serves one of these spiritual powers. So, whether you chose to 1) follow your own way apart from God or 2) follow God's way and learn His teaching, you are a slave to one spiritual power or the other. You can choose to be a slave to sin, which leads to empty living and death, or you can choose to be a slave to obeying God, which leads to the fullest and happiest living—having a life like God's.

[17]But thanks be to God, for once you used to be slaves to the sinful, spiritual power of this present age, but now your hearts are fully devoted and committed to obeying the full pattern of Jesus' teachings. [18]As a result, you have been set free from slavery to the sinful, spiritual power that is at work in this world. And you have become slaves to the godly, spiritual power that is at work in this world, the power which leads to a full and happy life and to right living with God.

[19]Because of our human limitations, I am using an example from everyday life to try and help you to understand this simultaneous reality of the Christian life—how God's grace and our actions work together. On one hand, through what God has done for us, He gives us this new life by His grace. On the other hand, through what we must chose to do, we grow into this new life of living in His grace. For just as you once offered your full self—all your knowledge, skills, abilities, motivations, and devotion—as slaves serving a sinful, spiritual power (which led to impurity of character and rebellion against God), so now offer your full self—all your knowledge, skills, abilities, motivations, and devotion—as slaves serving God's holy, spiritual power that is at work in this world. Serving God's holy power leads to developing more of a Christ-like character, which is the very life and character you were created to live and enjoy forever.

[20]For when you were once slaves to the sinful, spiritual power, you may have not have even realized it, but you were actually enslaved to and serving the authority of this present age. It may have felt like you were free from any obligation to anyone or anything, that you were free to determine your own sense of what was right. [21]But what did you gain from living this illusion that you were free from anyone's rule

or authority? You are now ashamed of those experiences and those mistaken choices and wrong behaviors. They were a dead-end spiritual street that did not lead to any lasting meaning, health, fullness of life, or joy in your soul.

[22]But now you have been set free from the influential rule of the sinful, spiritual power at work in the world. You have become slaves to God's new, spiritual power and authority. As a result, you choose to serve Him and do the things that develop more of a Christ-like character in you, the things that develop and promote your new life with God, the life that endures eternally in this new age.

[23]When you worked hard for the sinful, spiritual authority that is active in the world, your regular paycheck and eternal retirement plan was death (in every sense of the word). But under God's spiritual power and authority—where the new reign has already begun because of Jesus' resurrection—God gives you the gift of a regular paycheck of His grace and the new kind of life that endures eternally through Christ Jesus our Lord.

3.3 The new power of God working in people's lives frees them from the bondage of trying to earn our way to God (7:1-25).

> *3.3.1 Human beings are released from the non-life-giving standards of trying to keep the Old Covenant Law and joined to God's New Covenant of grace through Christ (7:1-6).*

CHAPTER 7

[1]As mentioned earlier, we no longer live under the burden of the old regime that required us to earn our way to God through keeping the Mosaic Law by trying to perfectly obey all the commands in the first five books of the Old Covenant Scripture [Old Testament]. Instead, we have now transitioned away from the burden of the old regime to live under the new regime of God's grace. My dear brothers and sisters, surely you understand this transition away from the old regime's

way of spiritual life, as you are very familiar with how the Mosaic Law works. For example, you surely know that the law only has power and authority over someone as long as that person lives, right?

²Let me illustrate this point. A married woman is bound by the law to her husband as long as he lives. But if her husband dies, then she is released and free from the law that binds her to him. ³If she lives with another man while her husband is alive, she will be called an adulteress. However, if her husband dies, she is free from that law and is not an adulteress if she marries another man. Death frees her from the power of the law.

⁴So then, my dear brothers and sisters, here is my point: By faith in Christ and through the death of His body, His death becomes yours. As such, you have died to the power of the old form of God's Mosaic Law. Like the woman freed from the law's requirements, you are no longer bound to the old regime of religious law. You are free to belong to another—more specifically, by faith, you are free to be united with Jesus who was raised from the dead. You have been freed from the old form of the law and are now bound to Christ for a new purpose: that you may bear fruit for God through useful service to Him.

⁵We used to live according to our sinful, human nature—which refers to when we lived in this world only focused on ourselves, motivated only by our own concerns and without any concern for God or our souls. When we lived life driven by our sinful, human nature, our sinful passions were awakened and stirred up by the old form of the law. These sinful passions and drives were constantly operating within our lives. And what was the result? We bore the fruit of death (in every sense of the word, but especially spiritually). ⁶But now we have been released and are free from this old regime of God's moral law. We have died to what constrained us and held us captive. Now, we have been set free to serve God—not in the outwardly focused way of obeying the written code of the Mosaic Law but in the inwardly motivated new way of obeying the Spirit.

3.3.2 Human beings recognize the problem of indwelling sin within them through the help of the Old Covenant Law (7:7-25).

SIN USES THE OLD COVENANT LAW TO MANIPULATE HUMAN BEINGS INTO TRYING TO BE RIGHT WITH GOD THROUGH THEIR OWN RELIGIOUS EFFORTS AND ACTIONS (7:7-12).

⁷What then shall we conclude about the Mosaic Law, the first five books of the Old Covenant Scriptures? Given everything I have said about the negative effects of trying to keep those commands and how everyone will fall short of them, I can hear someone asking: Are you saying that sin and the Mosaic Law are the same thing? Are you saying that the Mosaic Law of the Old Covenant is equal to and identical with sin? Given all that you have said about its negative effects, is not the Mosaic Law the real problem?

The blunt answer: Absolutely not! That is certainly not the case. The Mosaic Law is not sin nor the reason for sin, although there is a relationship between the two. So, what is that relationship? The Old Covenant Law helped me to come to understand the extent and seriousness of sin. I would not have understood what sin really is had it not been for the Old Covenant Law. For example, I would have not understood the true nature of coveting if the Old Covenant Law had not said, "You shall not engage your evil and wrong desires."

⁸But while the Mosaic Law helped me to understand what sin is, the sinful nature living inside of me seized the opportunity of me understanding God's command and used it against me. The sinful nature inside me used that awareness to produce all kinds of evil and wrong desires within me. For apart from God's moral law, sin would not be able to take advantage of my understanding as it currently does; it would not be able to use my awareness of God's standard to produce "forbidden fruit."

⁹I was once alive apart from an understanding of God's moral law and its expectations. But as soon as I learned about God's standards—His commandments and instructions for living—the power of sin sprang to life within me. As a result, my sinful choices and actions produced

death in me. [10]I discovered that the very commandments and words of instruction in the Old Covenant Law that were intended to bring life actually brought death. And who was to blame? Not God's Law or Scripture, but me. I am to blame, because I chose to follow the sinful nature working within me.

[11]Sin seized the opportunity of my understanding God's moral law as it is revealed in the Old Covenant. It deceived me into believing that because I intellectually understood God's moral law, I was somehow above sin affecting me. It deceived me into thinking that I could do what I was not supposed to do. It fooled me into believing that understanding God's truth was the same as living it, which is not the case. By giving in to my own sinful deception, sin operated as a personal, spiritual weapon working against my mind, body, and soul. It led me to death in the process. [12]So, do not think that God's moral law revealed in the Old Covenant is sinful. It is not! God's moral law revealed in the Old Covenant is holy; it is pure and morally perfect. Its commands and words of instruction are right and good.

THE OLD COVENANT LAW HELPS REVEAL THE PROBLEM OF SIN LIVING WITHIN HUMAN BEINGS (7:13-25).

[13]So, we just said that the Mosaic Law of the Old Covenant does not cause our violations of God's moral standard. Instead, God's moral standards revealed in the Mosaic Law are good. However, our sinful nature uses them to cause death in our lives. And I can almost hear your next question: Did God's revealed moral law cause our spiritual death? No way! Not by any means. The sin that lives within us caused it! Our sinful nature used what was good to produce death—in every type and form—in us. Our sinful nature uses God's good moral law, commands, and instructions for living to help us recognize how we rebel against God's ways. Then our sinful nature manipulates and deceives us into sinful practices, leading us to miss the mark of God's holy and perfect moral standard. Our sinful nature makes us utterly sinful—through and through and beyond any reasonable doubt. Even though our sinful nature is what makes us utterly sinful, God's commandments provide us with a mirror. They help us to see and recognize just how utterly sinful we really are.

[14]I want to clearly acknowledge what the problem is. The problem is not God's moral law. God's moral law is spiritually good. The problem lives within me; it lives within each one of us! For I have a sinful nature that is embedded in my human existence. It is as if my entire humanity has been sold into slavery under the power and control of sin. [15]As a result, I experience spiritual conflict within me, and I often do not understand my own actions. For my will and inner being wants to do what is right, but I end up not doing it. Instead, I end up doing the things I hate. [16]And who is responsible? Me! Since I know that what I am doing is wrong, it shows that the indwelling sin in me is responsible for my spiritual defeat. It also shows that my inner being knows and agrees that God's moral law is good. [17]But let us go a step further and realize where the deeper root of the problem is. The problem is that, even though I strive to follow Christ, the sinful nature still dwells inside of me! As a follower of Christ, it is not my new, true self doing these sinful things—that part of me is actively working to overcome them. Instead, it is the old, sinful self that still dwells within my inner being and lives within me.

[18]This is so important, so let me emphasize it again. I know that even all my good intentions and desires are tainted with sin and evil. I recognize that I am incapable of being morally perfect and turning all my good desires into good deeds. I acknowledge that it is the sin still dwelling within me and fighting for survival within my human nature that is the problem. And what is the result? I experience spiritual conflict in my life. I have the desire to do what is right in God's sight, but I am not able to do it. [19]I want to do what is good, but I do not do it. Instead, I keep on doing the wrong and the evil things I do not want to do. [20]And who is responsible? I am, because I choose to follow that part of my sinful nature that is fighting for survival within me. And I actually recognize it fighting for survival when I do the things I do not want to do. Yet, in those moments, I recognize that I am too powerless to do the good I want to do. I realize in those moments that my rebellious, sinful nature against God still has some power over me, and it fools me into doing those things I do not want to do.

[21]I have found that these two warring natures are consistently fighting for control of my life. I have found four ways they fight and war

within me. First, I have discovered them in two basic motivations that are trying to direct my actions. When I have the desire to do good within me, then rest assured, the desire to do evil is right there inside of me as well.

[22]Second, I also see these warring natures in the two moral laws that are trying to guide my life. In my inner being, I endorse and delight in God's moral law and His instructions for living. [23]But then I see another moral standard that is not of God at work trying to guide my life as well. It wages war against the good moral law in my mind and makes me a captive—a prisoner—of the law of sin that is still at work in my body.

[24]Third, I recognize these two warring natures in the two dispositions that are trying to control my heart. From within my old and sinful nature, I am powerless to live the life I want to be living. And my heart cries out, saying, "Oh, what an unhappy, worthless, inferior, inadequate, wretched, and hopeless person I am! Is there not anyone who can help me, fix me, and rescue me from this life that is dominated by this cycle of rebellion against God and death?" [25]But from within my new and Christ-like nature, I am empowered by God's grace to live the life I want to be living. And my heart cries out, saying, "Thanks be to the God who has answered my soul's dilemma and who delivers me through Jesus Christ our Lord!"

Fourth, I realize that there are two different masters trying to guide my life. With my mind, I am slave to and serve God's instructions for living. But it seems it is only with my mind that I can serve Him, because I have a sinful, human nature at work within me. That oppressive nature works to make me a slave and servant to the moral law of sin, which allows sin to guide and direct my life.

3.4 The new power of God working in peoples' lives gives them the assurance of eternal life in the Spirit (8:1-30).

3.4.1 The Spirit fills people with God's new kind of life (8:1-13).

CHAPTER 8

THE SPIRIT EMPHASIZES THE FREEDOM FROM CONDEMNATION THAT HUMAN BEINGS HAVE THROUGH CHRIST (8:1).

¹We have talked about the Old Covenant Law's powerlessness to make us right with God. We have expressed how our human sinful nature wars against us, making us incapable of living the Christian life apart from God's power. But in light of everything we have been talking about, let us realize that there is now no condemnation for those who belong to Christ Jesus. God does not assign any guilt of any wrongdoing to those who live and walk with Christ.

THE SPIRIT BRINGS NEW MOTIVATIONS AND FREEDOM (8:2-4).

²Why? Because you belong to Christ Jesus through faith. Through faith in Christ, the power of the new, life-giving law of the Spirit has liberated you. Your faith in Christ has set you free from the old era of attempting in vain to perfectly obey the Old Covenant moral law in order to be right with God. And, as we mentioned before, you cannot perfectly obey the Old Covenant moral standards anyway, and trying to find God via that path ultimately leads to death (in every sense of the word).

³Realize that, through faith in Christ, God has changed you! For God has done what the Old Covenant Law of Moses was powerless to accomplish: He has given you freedom from trying to earn God's favor and brought you into a New Covenant relationship with Himself. The Old Covenant moral standards were weakened by our innate, human, sinful nature; they did not have the power to free us. But God has accomplished our freedom from sin's power. He has freed us from the guilt associated with our rebellion against God by sending His own Son. He sent His own Son in the likeness of sinful flesh (meaning that Christ had a fully human body that experienced the effects of being in a fallen world). And His Son, fully existing in the likeness of our

human existence, was given as a sacrificial sin offering, meaning that His blood covers over and pays the price for our sins. Through this sacrificial offering for our sin, God was able to fully judge and completely condemn human rebellion against His ways and the violations of His moral law by putting it to death in body of Jesus.

[4]God put Jesus' body to death in order that the just requirement of God's moral law and standards might be fully met in us, and that we would be morally pure and without any fault. And not only has the price of death been paid for our sins, but through faith, we now live a new kind of life through Christ's resurrection! We no longer live a life governed by, motivated by, and seeking to follow our sinful nature. Instead, we are now governed, motivated by, and seeking to follow the Spirit.

THE SPIRIT CHANGES ATTITUDES AND MINDSETS (8:5-8).

[5]God has given us a new status with Him; He has given us a new freedom via His life-giving Spirit. His life-giving Spirit motivates our lives now, but here is a crucial point about His rule in our lives: Our mindset matters because it reveals our true nature. Those whose lives are dominated by their old, sinful nature have their minds set on a variety of things of this world. Their minds are without any care or concern for God. However, those whose lives are motivated and controlled by the Holy Spirit have their minds set on the things that please the Spirit.

[6]Our mindset has eternal consequences. The mind governed by, motivated by, and seeking to follow our human, sinful nature results in death (spiritual death now, eternal death later). However, the mind governed, motivated by, and seeking to follow the Spirit results in life and peace (spiritual life and peace now, eternal life and peace later).

[7]Our mindset also reveals our attitude toward God. For the mind that is set on the pursuits of our human, sinful nature is hostile to God. That sinful mindset is working for itself with no care or concern for Him. It does not submit to or obey God's moral law, nor will it do so. [8]That is why those whose minds are governed by, motivated by, and seeking to follow the sinful nature of humanity cannot please God.

THE SPIRIT INDWELLS—LIVING AND WORKING WITHIN—THOSE WHO HAVE FAITH IN CHRIST (8:9-13).

⁹But here is a fact and a reality you must comprehend: You no longer belong to the sinful, spiritual power of this present age, which is dominated by our sinful nature. Instead, you now below to the godly, spiritual power of a new age that has come through Christ. As a result, you, as a follower of Christ, are not governed by, motivated by, and seeking to follow the sinful nature that lives within you. Instead, you are governed by, motivated by, and seeking to follow the Holy Spirit who now lives inside you. And if anyone does not have the Spirit of Christ living within them, then they do not belong to Christ.

¹⁰Having the Holy Spirit dwelling within you is a distinguishing mark of God's people, and it has two major effects on your life. First, the Spirit gives you and fills you with a new kind of life. For if Christ lives within you (as He certainly does, since you have faith in Him), then even though your mortal body is dying and will die (because of the effect of sin in a fallen world), the Holy Spirit gives and fills you with new life. The Holy Spirit gives you this new life because you have been brought into a right relationship with God.

¹¹But how can you be sure? Because if the Spirit of God who raised Jesus from the dead lives within you (as He certainly does since you have faith in Him), then just as God raised Christ Jesus from the dead, He will also give life to you in a new, resurrected body. God will give life to your new body through His Spirit who lives within you.

¹²Second, the Spirit calls you to fulfill your responsibility to your new godly, spiritual ruler and authority. You are now part of the family of God, and that membership comes with responsibilities. Your responsibility—or family obligation—is not to the old, sinful, spiritual power, to that sinful nature that lies within humanity. You are not to live according to the sinful nature's influence. ¹³For if you live governed by, motivated by, and seeking to follow it, you will die. But if, through the power of the Spirit, you keep putting to death the deeds prompted by the sinful fibers of your existence, then you will live (in every sense of the word).

3.4.2 The Spirit helps people recognize that they have been fully adopted into God's family, and to realize that they will inherit all He has for them (8:14-17).

¹⁴The indwelling Spirit also helps you to know that you are not just under a new ruler, spiritual power, or authority, but that you are a child who belongs to God's family. For all those who are led by the Spirit of God are the children of God. ¹⁵And you did not receive a half-hearted membership into God's family. No, you did not receive a spirit that makes you a slave again to fear. Instead, you received God's Spirit when He adopted you into His family. This carries the same concept as adoption in the Roman world, where an adopted son was deliberately chosen to fully perpetuate the father's name, family line, and family character. The adopted one would inherit all that the father had. The adopted son's status was the same as if he had been born naturally from within the family. The adopted one enjoyed the fullness of the father's affection so that he might fully carry on the family's character. When you received God's Spirit within you, this is the kind of adoption you received into God's family. Because of that adoption and by the Spirit's power, we are able to call out to God in joyous, childlike enthusiasm and excitement, addressing Him in personal terms. We can call the God of all creation "Dad" and "our Father."

¹⁶When we call out to God in such direct and personal terms, it is the Spirit Himself that shares a strong, inward witness with our spirit that we are the children of God. ¹⁷And what is the result of our adoption? Since we are fully God's children, we are also His heirs. Together with Christ, we are heirs who will share in the richest, fullest, deepest, and most valuable inheritance in all existence—God's glory! God's glory, which we inherit, is so far beyond comprehension that words cannot fully convey its greatness! And we can be certain that if we share in Christ's sufferings, then we will also share in His glory.

3.4.3 The Spirit helps people to have perspective on their present suffering and to realize the reality of future joy and glory with God (8:18-30).

[18]The experience of suffering and glory are both parts of our lives as followers of Christ. But when I think about them, I realize they belong to two vastly different ages: one to this present age that is under the influence of sin, the other to God's new age that has come through Christ. However, one of these ages is so vastly superior to the other that there is actually no comparison to be made between the two. In that light, our present sufferings are not even worth comparing to the all-surpassing greatness of the glory of God that will be revealed to us. [19]Yet, in our present life and reality, this tension between suffering and glory continues. And in the present, the tension between suffering and glory is not just ours alone. It relates to both God's children and His creation. For the created universe—including the earth and all it contains—waits with eager expectation (as though it is trying to stand on tiptoes and stretch its neck to see over a fence, or like it is squinting to see what is coming on the horizon). It eagerly awaits for God to fully reveal His glory in His children.

[20]Why? Because creation was also subjected to frustration, futility, purposelessness, and emptiness when sin entered the created world. These things happened to creation not by its own choice. They happened as a result of human rebellion against God, and human sinfulness brought a state of fallenness and brokenness to the world (which God warned would happen). But with eager hope, [21]creation looks forward to the coming day of its liberation. On that coming day, two things will happen. First, it will be liberated from its captivity to an endless cycle of birth and decline, decay, death, and decomposition. Second, it will be brought into and share in what God's children will have: the fullness of God's freedom and His glory.

[22]For we know that the entire created universe has been groaning as in the pains of childbirth, right up to this present day. It groans while waiting for the liberating transformation that will come through Christ. [23]And during this experience of present suffering and coming glory, creation is not alone in its groaning. God's children also share

in this tension between suffering and glory. We have the Holy Spirit within us as a foretaste of the future glory to come (the first installment of our full inheritance). Yet we still groan inwardly as we eagerly wait for our full rights and inheritance as God's adopted children. When we receive our full inheritance from God, it will include new, redeemed, and resurrected bodies that will no longer experience any form of suffering.

[24]Through faith in Christ, we were given this hope. But this hope is just the first piece of sand in an endless ocean that is yet to be seen. If we could fully see everything we are waiting for now, then that would not really be hope. After all, who hopes for what they already have? [25]But if we are eagerly anticipating and looking forward to seeing the whole picture of God's full glory—the picture that we do not yet fully have or see—then we wait for it with confident patience.

[26]In the same way that the indwelling Holy Spirit gives us freedom and new life, He also helps us live right here as well. He helps us live in the midst of the tension between our present sufferings and our future glory with God. Here is an example of how the Holy Spirit helps us: We do not always know what God wants us to pray for, but the Spirit prays for us with groans that cannot be put into words. [27]And the great thing about Him praying on our behalf is that God the Father, the One who searches our hearts, knows the mind of the Spirit. And the Spirit speak with God on behalf of His people, and He pleads for God's people in harmony with God's will.

3.5 The new power of God working in peoples' lives can be celebrated because nothing can ever separate those who have faith in Christ from the love of God (8:31-39).

[28]In the first part of this letter, I discussed how we are justified by faith. Since the beginning of this second part of the letter, I have been talking about two themes that are a result of our being made right with God: 1) how God's people can be assured of our final salvation, and 2) how the new power that God gives us helps us in our struggle against trying to perfectly obey the Old Covenant moral law and against the

sinful nature that leads us to rebel against God's moral standard. But now, I want to shift our focus. I want to elevate your minds as high as I possibly can, so that you might be certain of the eternal security God's people have. Specifically, I want you to have three experiences in connection with God's bigger plan and greater purpose:

1) be convinced of the bigger picture of how God works in our lives,
2) see the stages through which God achieves our salvation, and
3) ponder a series of questions that will help us settle the matter in our hearts and minds.

First, let us look at the big picture of how God works in our lives.

3.5.1 Those who have faith in Christ have five certainties about how God works in their lives (8:28b).

There are five things we can be certain about in connection with how God works in our lives:

1) We know God is energetically and purposefully at work in our lives and does not stop.
2) We know God is at work in our lives for our spiritual and holistic good.
3) We know God is for our good in all things. Through all the good, bad, and ugly moments of life, God is achieving the positive purpose of our salvation, which also plays into His larger, eternal plans.
4) We know God works for the good of our salvation in all things. He works in this way for all those who love Him. His good is openly offered and available to all, but only those who love Him will know and experience it fully.
5) We know that God is working in the lives of those who love Him, because they have been called by Him. Life is not a random mess of chance events and happenings for those He has called. God has called them, and He is working in their lives for His purpose.

3.5.2 Those who have faith in Christ can know the five stages through which God achieves their salvation (8:29-30).

[29]Second, knowing that God's purpose for working in our lives is for our good (meaning our salvation), let us now look at five stages through which God achieves that purpose.

1) Those God personally foreknew, He foreloved by choosing them to be His people—for them to be the ones He would care for, watch over, and work in.

2) Those God foreknew, He decided beforehand and predestined that they would be conformed to the likeness of His Son—having a character just like Jesus'—so that Jesus might be the firstborn among a larger family of God's children who all share His character.

3) [30]Those God decided on beforehand and predestined, He also called out to them and awakened their faith.

4) Those God called out to, He also justified, declaring them not guilty of any wrongdoing and looking at them as though they had never done anything wrong.

5) Those God justified, He also glorified, giving them a foretaste now of what they are assured to one day receive when He gives them His full glory in heaven.

3.5.3 Those who have faith in Christ can ponder five questions that help settle the matter of salvation in their hearts (8:31-37).

[31]Third, considering these five certainties about how God works in our lives and the five stages through which He achieves our salvation, what else really needs to be said? But let us continue to explore these wonders by contemplating five questions that help settle the matter in our hearts.

1) If God—the highest, most powerful, and most loving being in the entire universe—is for us, who can possibly be against us?

2) ³²If God loved us so much that He did not spare His own Son (His greatest gift), but graciously gave Him up to save us, how can He possibly fail to graciously give us every other good gift in glory?

3) ³³Since God has already justified us—declaring us not guilty of any wrongdoing and seeing us as fully right in His sight—who can possibly bring any charge or accusation of unrighteousness against us, the ones God has chosen?

4) ³⁴Since God has not condemned us for our wrongdoing and unrighteousness, who then can possibly overrule God to condemn us? No one can, for Christ Jesus—the One who died and was raised to life for us—is sitting in His place of power and honor at God's right hand. From that place of power, He intercedes with God the Father on our behalf.

5) ³⁵Can anyone or anything ever separate us from the love of Christ? If we are experiencing pressure or distress in the world, having trouble, encountering hardship, being persecuted, or going hungry, does that mean Christ no longer loves us? If there are things we lack in life such as facing a widespread famine or having to go naked because we do not have clothes, does that mean Christ no longer loves us? What if we encounter danger or are confronted by death from an executioner's sword? ³⁶Does not Scripture warn us that we will face danger? As it is written in Psalm 43:22: "For your sake, God, we face death all day long; we are treated like sheep that are going to be slaughtered." If we are confronted by danger and death like this, does that mean Christ no longer loves us? ³⁷No way! Even while we are enduring all of these things, we are triumphing over them as conquerors and winning a most glorious victory through Christ Jesus who loves us.

3.5.4 Those who have faith in Christ cannot be separated from the love of God (8:38-39).

[38]For I have become and remain convinced that neither the crisis of death nor the calamities of life; neither cosmic, spiritual forces for good (angels) nor spiritual forces for bad (demons); neither our fears in the present nor our worries about the future; not any of the powers or forces at work in the universe; [39]neither any astrological power in the skies above nor in the earth below—nor anything else in all creation will ever be able to separate us from the love of God that is in Christ Jesus our Lord.

4. God has been working through the past, present, and future to fulfill His promise and form a global community of people who belong to Him and reflect His character (9:1–11:36).

4.1 The issue: Given the tension between God's promises to Israel in the Old Covenant and their current rejection of God's New Covenant revealed in Christ, does that mean that God cannot be trusted to keep His promises? (9:1-5)

CHAPTER 9

[1]In light of the great reality that nothing can separate a follower of Christ from the great love of God, I want to shift gears. I want you to see how this gospel of God—a gospel that says we are made right with God through Christ—is one single message with His revelation in the Old Covenant [Old Testament]. I want you to see how God's work has been consistent throughout history. Since the Jewish people, who had the Old Covenant, failed to recognize their Messiah, and since the non-Jewish Gentiles now make up the majority group of God's people, it is vital to understand that God has not changed. Both God's character and His message are consistent. Or to phrase it in the form of a question, "Can God be trusted to do what He says?" Simply and plainly stated, the answer is yes!

Now let us dig deeper and explore what appears to be a tension between God's promises about the coming Messiah (who is the Christ) to the people of Israel in the Old Covenant and their present refusal to recognize or believe in Christ Jesus. However, before we do, I want to share my personal thoughts about this matter with you. I know some people like to think I am a Jewish traitor, so I want to tell you the truth about how I feel very clearly. With Christ as my witness, through the Holy Spirit living in me, and with every fiber of my conscience confirming it, I am not lying about the true feelings I have for you.

²My heart is filled tremendous sorrow and endless grief over the people of Old Covenant Israel, for they are not recognizing and believing in Christ Jesus. ³If my own personal destruction had a chance of saving the people of my own race (the Israelites), then I would wish I could be forever cursed and cut off from Christ in order help them. But that is not how it works. They must make their own decisions.

⁴It is a sad situation because they are the very people God chose to work through in the Old Covenant. It utterly and completely amazes me that my fellow Jewish people had eight great religious privileges to lead them to recognize Christ, yet so many of them still rejected Him. These religious privileges included:

1) As a nation, they were chosen to be God's adopted children.
2) God has revealed His glory—His ultimate value and worth—to them throughout history.
3) God made lasting covenants and promises with them, giving them the assurance that He would never break His word.
4) He gave them the revelation of His moral law—His words of instruction and guidance on how to live.
5) They were able to worship God in the Temple, which symbolically represented His presence among them and also foreshadowed how God's people would eventually experience His full, immersed, and actual presence living among them.
6) They received God's promise of what was yet to come.

7) ⁵They had the ancestry of the religious patriarchs in Genesis (Abraham, Isaac, Jacob, and Joseph), which connected them to the family line of those whom had received God's promises from the beginning.

8) From their lineage and race, the human ancestry of Jesus Christ can be traced—the Lord, who is God over all and worthy to be praised forever! Amen.

The people of Israel had so many religious privileges! These privileges should have led them to receive Christ, yet so many of them have not believed in Him.

4.2 In the past, God worked through the Old Covenant nation of Israel to form a spiritual people who would belong to Him and be prepared to receive Christ (9:6-29).

> *4.2.1 God called and formed a new, spiritual Israel who genuinely belonged to Him within the Old Covenant people of Israel (9:6-13).*

⁶Now, let us revisit our current question: Since God was working through the Jewish people in the Old Covenant, and since they failed to recognize the Messiah, can God be trusted to do what He says? Let me again state my answer very clearly: The promises that God has spoken in the past have not failed! The God of the Old Covenant Scripture is the same God of the New Covenant gospel of Christ. God is faithful, and He is reliable throughout history. How God is working in the world is consistent with what He did in the past, regardless of whether the Jewish people fail to recognize their Messiah.

So that you can see how the words of God's promises have not failed and that He has always been reliable, let us first state a plain fact about God's work, and then look at two examples of that fact at work.

PLAIN FACT ABOUT GOD'S WORK: GOD'S PEOPLE ARE DETERMINED BY SPIRITUAL DYNAMICS AND SPIRITUAL REALITIES (9:6B-7A).

The plain fact is this: God's people are not determined by racial, physical, or religious heritage but by spiritual dynamics and realities. While many Jewish people like to think that racial, physical, and religious heritage makes them right with God, here is the plain truth about the Israelites—about the ones who are supposed to be the people of God. The truth is that there are two Israels: one physical, the other spiritual. And God has always chosen some from the "physical" nation of Israel to be part of His true "spiritual" people.

⁷The Jewish people like to focus on their physical connection to Abraham. They like to think their racial, national, and family ancestry provides them with the all the relationship to God they need to be right with Him. However, even though they like to think such things, being a physical descendant of Abraham has never determined who God's genuine, spiritual children really are, nor has it provided people with the kind of substantive and ongoing relationship they truly need with God. Throughout the history of the Old Covenant, there have always been two Israels: one relying on physical realities and the other relying on spiritual realities. God has always chosen who His children are, those who would receive His promise of salvation. God's promise has never been based on mere physical connection but on spiritual dynamics. So, that is the plain fact about God's work: God's children come not from physical descendants but by spiritual realities, as they are chosen by God.

Now, let us look at our first example of this plain fact at work.

EXAMPLE ONE: GOD CHOSE TO CARRY FORWARD HIS PROMISE THROUGH ISAAC, THE UNEXPECTED CHILD BORN EVEN WHEN IT SEEMED PHYSICALLY IMPOSSIBLE (9:7B-10A).

Our first example comes from the patriarchs of the Old Covenant. In it, we learn that God has been choosing who His true spiritual offspring are from the beginning. In Genesis 21:12, we see God choosing who belongs to Him when He says to Abraham, "It is through Isaac that your offspring will be called and counted," even though Abraham had other children who were not chosen.

⁸This scripture teaches us that the true children of God are not determined by physical descent. Instead, the true children of God are the ones who have been called and chosen to receive His promise

of salvation. Those called and chosen by God are the ones who are counted as Abraham's true spiritual descendants. [9]It is also clear that God's promise was carried on by His gracious intervention. We see this when God said to Abraham in Genesis 18:10, "At the appointed time, I will return, and Sarah will have a son." [10]And that is not the only example where we see God choosing who will receive His promise of salvation (a salvation that does not rely on a psychical connection but a spiritual dynamic).

EXAMPLE TWO: GOD CHOSE TO CARRY HIS PROMISE FORWARD THROUGH JACOB, THE SECOND CHILD, RATHER THAN ISAAC'S FIRSTBORN (9:10B-13).

Our second example comes from the son who was born to Sarah in our first example: Isaac, another one of our spiritual forefathers. When Isaac married Rebekah, both of her children were conceived at the same time. [11]But before the twins were born or had done anything good or bad of their own, Rebekah received a message from God. The message she received demonstrates how God chooses people according to His purposes. [12]Even though it was natural and the norm in that culture for the firstborn to receive the family inheritance and carry on the family's promise, God chose to reverse the order. God told Rebekah in Genesis 25:23, "Your older son will serve your younger son." [13]By God's own decision, He chose to carry forth His plan and promise through the younger son, Jacob. It had nothing to do with Jacob's individual efforts or personal merit; it was the spiritual dynamic of God's choosing and God's work that made it happen. Hundreds of years later, recognizing how God had graciously worked through Jacob to carry forth His promises, it was written in Malachi 1:2-3, "Jacob I loved, but Esau I rejected."

> *4.2.2 God is not unfair or unjust in choosing who belongs to Him. God is free to do whatever He desires with His creatures and creation (9:14-23).*

[14]Since we have clearly said that God freely chooses and calls who will be His true offspring, I can almost hear a very natural question coming to your mind: If our salvation is not based on what we do but is determined by God's divine choice, is it not unfair and unjust for God

to act that way toward us, for Him to be "selective?" The short answer: No way! Not by any means!

¹⁵Throughout human history, God has freely acted this way. For example, God said to Moses in Exodus 33:19, "I will have mercy on whomever I chose, and I will have compassion on whomever I decide." ¹⁶Throughout the Scriptures of the Old Covenant, we see God acting consistently to choose whom He will show mercy on and whom He will not. His choice does not depend on human desire and cannot be earned or influenced by our efforts.

¹⁷Even when God chooses not to show His mercy on others, He is acting freely and consistently, acting by His divine choice. We see an example of this in Exodus 9:16 when God says to Pharaoh, "I have raised you up for this very purpose, that I might display My power in you. By doing so, the character of My power and existence might be known and proclaimed throughout all the earth."

¹⁸Throughout human history, God chooses to have mercy on some, and He chooses to leave others with their hard hearts—hearts that are already in a state of insensitivity toward Him, His Word, and His work in the world. God is not being unjust if He leaves people in their hardened state of insensitivity to Him. Instead, God shows us mercy by choosing to call any of us into a right relationship with Himself through faith in Christ.

¹⁹Since God's divine choice decides to whom He will show mercy, I can almost hear another question coming to your mind: "Since God's divine choice decides whom He will show mercy to, then why does God still blame us for not responding to Him? Are not those who refuse to believe simply doing what He has chosen for them to do?"

²⁰That may sound like a rational question, but you are forgetting who God is. He is the Supreme Being of the universe, the One of whom there is none higher. So, who do you think you are? Who are you, as a mere human being, to talk back and argue with God's desires? Should the thing that is created say to the One who created it, "Why have You made me this way?" ²¹When the potter makes jars from the clay,

does he not have the freedom and right to make what he wants from the clay—deciding to make some vessels for honor, some for special purposes, and other vessels for consumable and common use?

²²Even when we accept that God chooses to show His just wrath and make His power known on those who are destined for destruction, we may wonder why He does it. Or we may wonder why He takes so long to do it. But what if you are looking at it the wrong way? What if God "takes His time" in order to demonstrate just how amazing His love and patience are toward the objects who are deserving of His wrath, those who are destined for destruction? ²³What if God is "taking His time" because He wants to make the all-surpassing riches of His great worth known to the objects who are receiving His mercy? What if He is being patient to help those whom He is preparing for future glory to better understand and appreciate now His full glory that awaits them?

> 4.2.3 God foretold that He would call a new, spiritual people
> to belong to Him. They are formed not by national,
> personal, racial, social, or any other factors but by His
> calling and grace (9:24-29).

²⁴And what if we are these people—the ones God is preparing for His future glory? What if we were the ones deserving of God's wrath, but instead of receiving His wrath, we are now among those whom God has chosen and called? Because God has called us, we are now people who have received His mercy. ²⁵God has called everyone, whether Jew or Gentile, to belong to Him regardless of their racial or religious backgrounds. And His calling is consistent with His work in the past. In the Scriptures of the Old Covenant, we see that God speaks about how He will call the Gentiles to Himself. In Hosea chapter 2, God says, "I will call those who were not racially or physically recognized as my people to enter into a relationship with me that identifies them as my people. The nations, the ones that seem disconnected from me, will now know and experience the full affection of my love."

²⁶Again, in Hosea 1, we see that God shows no distinction between Jews and Gentiles when He says, "In the very land and places where

they were told, 'You are not God's people,' they will be called 'the children of the living god.' The people in these seemingly disconnected lands will have a social status like a son in our culture, where they will inherit everything."

²⁷Also, in the Old Covenant Scriptures, we see that not everyone who is a physical or racial Jew belongs to God. We see God calling out a spiritual people even from those physically identified as the nation of Israel, calling out those of faith who genuinely belong to Him. ¹⁰In the book of Isaiah, we hear God speaking through Isaiah the prophet, saying, "Even though the people of Israel are as numerous as the sand by the sea, yet only a remnant—a small part of them—will be saved. ²⁸For the Lord will carry out the sentence of His judgment on the earth quickly and with finality."

²⁹Again, in Isaiah 1, we see God saying that only a remnant—a small part—of the Jewish people will truly belong to Him. There, Isaiah predicted, "If the Almighty Lord of Heaven's Armies had not left us some of His genuine, spiritual offspring, we would have been demolished like Sodom and destroyed like Gomorrah."

4.3 In the present, Old Covenant Israel is missing out on what God is doing through Christ (9:30–10:21).

> *4.3.1 Since Old Covenant Israel has stumbled by failing to have faith in Christ, and since the Gentiles have not stumbled and believe, it may appear to be an upside-down world (9:30-33).*

³⁰Since God had been working through the Israelites throughout history to prepare the way for the Messiah, and since they missed God's work when He arrived and failed to respond to Him, what then shall we conclude from all of this? Everything may seem a bit upside-down. On the one hand, the Gentiles were not trying to follow Gods' standard or to be made right with Him. However, they have now obtained it and been brought into a right relationship with God through faith. ³¹On the other hand, the people of Israel were trying hard to be right

with God. They thought they could make themselves right with God through their own efforts to obey and keep the moral expectations of the Mosaic Law in the Old Covenant. However, they failed to realize they were pursuing an impossible goal, and so they failed to obtain it. So, everything may seem to be religiously upside-down, that those who were trying so hard to have a right relationship with God not only failed to obtain it but also have become the minority group among those who are His people.

³²But why did this seemingly upside-down spiritual situation happen? How did the people of Israel fail in their goal? Because they did not pursue being made right with God through faith. Instead, they trusted in their own works, actions, and efforts as the path to a right relationship with God. They stumbled over the stumbling stone that was foretold in the Old Covenant. ³³As God said to them in Isaiah 28:16, "Pay attention to what I am doing. I am placing a Stone in Jerusalem that makes people stumble, a Rock that makes them fall." And He said to them in Isaiah 8:14, "Whoever believes in Him—this Rock—will never be disgraced, disappointed, or unable to find their way."

4.3.2 Many people from Old Covenant Israel have failed to recognize God's New Covenant work in Christ (10:1-13).

CHAPTER 10

¹Since the people of Israel stumbled over the stumbling stone and have been relying on their own efforts to keep the Old Covenant law in order be right with God, they need the gospel of God. My dear brothers and sisters, I hope you know of my passion for the people of Israel. I long for them to be saved. Their salvation is my heart's desire and my prayer to God. ²And I must long for their salvation with all my heart and with my prayers, for I was once like them. I can testify from first-hand experience about how zealous they are in their pursuit for God. However, I can also testify from first-hand experience that their zeal is misdirected; it is not based on full spiritual knowledge.

³Their misdirected zeal and lack of full, spiritual knowledge can be clearly seen in the way they failed to see what God was doing through

Christ. They did not understand or accept God's way of righteousness when it was revealed to them—God's way of making people
right with Himself through faith in Christ. Instead, they insisted on
seeking a relationship with God based on their own self-determined
terms. They clung to their own way of trying to make themselves right
with God by trying to keep His moral law and by trusting in their
own efforts to earn His approval.

⁴They failed to realize that seeking their own way of trying make
themselves right with God is wrong. They have failed to recognize that
Christ is the culmination of God's moral law and expectations—the
climactic and decisive turning point within the history of God's plan
for salvation. Since Christ has already accomplished and fulfilled the
purpose of the Old Covenant moral law, He has now made a way of
being right with God that is available to everyone who believes.

> 4.3.3 The path to salvation is through faith, but many people
>   from Old Covenant Israel choose not to believe in Christ
>   (10:5-13).

⁵The scriptures of the Old Covenant [Old Testament] contrast these
two approaches for how people seek a right relationship with God.
We see the first approach mentioned in the teachings of Moses, where
he writes in Leviticus 18:5: "The person who wants to live [meaning
to be right with God by keeping the moral law of the Old Covenant]
must live in perfect obedience to all of its commands." In this scripture, we see that this first approach fails because it is attempting to
be right with God by trying to perfectly practice the Old Covenant
moral law, which simply cannot be done.

⁶However, we see a second approach mentioned in the Old Covenant
scriptures. This second approach is God's way of making us right with
Him through faith in Christ. God says in Deuteronomy 9:4, "Do not
say in your heart, 'Who will ascend into heaven and relate to God
on His level for us?'" (as this overlooks the reality of Christ's incarna-
tion—His leaving God the Father in heaven to come down to earth to
dwell among us as a fully-embodied human being) ⁷"and do not say,
'Who will descend into the depths of hell to defeat death, evil, and

the devil for us?'" (as this overlooks the reality of Christ's resurrection from the dead where He won the victory over these enemies).

[8]But what does God say in Deuteronomy 30:14? He says, "The message that saves is very close to you; it is in your mouth and in your heart." This is the message of God's salvation through faith that we are proclaiming: [9]If you declare outwardly with your mouth, "Jesus is Lord," and build your life around inwardly believing in your heart that God raised Him from the dead, you will be saved. [10]For it is by inwardly believing in your heart—believing in the core of who you are and in the part of you that orients and motivates your life—that you are justified, that you have been declared not guilty of violating God's moral standard and put into a right relationship with Him. And it is with your mouth that you outwardly profess your faith in Christ and are saved.

[11]The scriptures of the Old Covenant teach us this path to salvation. In Isaiah 28:16 it says, "Everyone who believes in Him will never be disgraced, disappointed, or unable to find their way." [12]And when it says "everyone," God means everyone, for there is no distinction in His sight between those of Jewish or Gentile backgrounds. The same God over one group of those who trust in Christ is the same Lord over all of them, and He gives generously to all who call on Him. [13]Scripture emphasizes that God's grace and unmerited favor are available to all in Joel 2:32, where it says, "Everyone who calls on the name of the Lord will be saved."

> 4.3.4 People from Old Covenant Israel have heard God's
>   message through Christ and are responsible for their
>   rejection of Him (10:14-21).

[14]Through Christ, God's grace and salvation are available to everyone. The people of Israel are responsible for rejecting Christ and not responding to God's call to believe in Him. To see how people are responsible for their own unbelief, let us start with God's calling and count backwards to see the steps—at least from a human perspective—in how people fail to respond to the gospel:

4) How can they call on Christ to save them if they have not believed in Him?

3) How can they believe in Christ if they have never heard about Him?

2) How can they hear about Christ unless someone tells them?

1) [15]How can anyone go and tell them unless they are sent?

Thankfully, God has sent His messengers to tell them. It is just as it is written in Isaiah 52, where the city was desolate and being held in captivity. They were in desperate need of the Lord's favor. And then in Isaiah 52:7, we see how some eagerly welcomed God's messengers and accepted their message, "How beautiful is the timely arrival of those who bring the good news of God's truth and salvation!"

[16]But even though they were all in a desolate and hopelessly dreadful situation, not all the Israelites welcomed or accept God's good news. The prophet Isaiah highlights in 53:1 how some of the Israelites continued in their unbelief when he says, "Lord, who has believed our message?" [17]But regardless of how people choose to respond, the process is clear: Faith comes from hearing God's truth, and His message of salvation is heard only when someone tells them the message about Christ. [18]As we think about the people of Israel, have they not heard God's message? Of course they have. As it says in Psalm 19:4: "God's voice has gone out into all the earth, and His words to the ends of world."

[19]But let me ask you again and explore this more deeply: Did the people of Israel really understand what they were hearing about God's salvation—that it would be available for all? Yes, the span of history in the Old Covenant's scriptures shows they understood the universal scope of God's salvation. First, during the time of Moses, in Deuteronomy 32:21, God said, "I will make you jealous of those people who are not of the nation of Israel. I will provoke your anger through the nations of the Gentiles whom you think are foolish and have no understanding." [20]Later on, God spoke boldly about how the Gentiles would find Him. In Isaiah 65:1, God says through the prophet Isaiah: "I have been found by those who did not seek Me; I have shown myself to those who did not ask for Me." [21]And God

also indicated how Israel would stubbornly reject Him when He says in Isaiah 65:2: "All day long I have held out My hands of grace to a people who are consistently disobedient, stubbornly rebellious, and steadily set against me."

4.4 Even though the people of Old Covenant Israel are missing out on God's work in the present, God is still at work forming a global, spiritual community of people who belong to Him (11:1-10).

CHAPTER 11

¹So, what does all of this mean right now for the nation and people of Old Covenant Israel? It is clear that Israel—the people God was preparing to be His own—has stumbled over a crucified Christ. They have turned from God's way of putting people into a right standing with Himself. Even though they had the tremendous opportunity of knowing God, they clearly missed out on that opportunity. They failed to recognize what God was doing through Christ. But since they missed what God was doing through Christ in the past, does that mean God has rejected all the people of Israel in the present?

In short: No way, absolutely not! In case you need evidence that God is still working in the Israelite people, just look at me! I am an Israelite, a descendant of Abraham, a member of the tribe of Benjamin. And God has called me to faith in Christ! ²No, God has not rejected His people, those whom He foreknew and chose to be His.

God choosing individuals in the present and calling them to faith from within a larger group of people is not new. It is in the Old Covenant scriptures. Do you not remember what the scripture says in 1 Kings 19 about Elijah? During a time when the prophets were being slaughtered by an unjust Israelite King, Elijah appeals to God to work against the people of Israel. He says, ³"Lord, they have killed your prophets and demolished the altars [the ones used during the time of the Old Covenant to connect people to God]. I am the only one left, and they are trying to kill me too!"

⁴But do you remember what God said to Him? He said, "You may feel like you are the only one left, but my work is bigger than what you can see and feel. I have kept 7,000 other people for Myself, people who have not bowed the knee in worship to the false god Baal."

⁵Just as a small part of the people of Israel remained faithful in the past (because of God's grace at work in them), in the same way, there is a remnant of faithful ones in the present who have been chosen by God's grace as well. ⁶Let me elaborate on this point: God freely chose these people, and they remain faithful to Him because God chose them. God did not choose them because of any good deeds they had done. They have not earned any credit or merit in God's sight. If that had been the case (that they could have earned their way to God), then God's choice would no longer be real grace, receiving His undeserved kindness that is given freely by His choosing.

⁷So, what should we conclude then about the present situation of the people of Israel? The sad reality is this: Even though the people of Old Covenant Israel had tremendous religious advantages and had an opportunity to respond to Christ, most of the people of Israel have failed to obtain the right standing with God they have been so earnestly seeking. A few among them—those God called—found a right standing with Him through faith in Christ; the rest became callously hardened in their spiritual blindness, indifference, and unresponsiveness.

⁸In every major section of the Old Covenant scriptures, which are the Law, Prophets, and Writings, we find people hardened against God. In the "Law" section of the Old Covenant, in Deuteronomy 29:4, and in the "Prophets," in Isaiah 29:10, it is written: "God gave them minds that were spiritually dull and unable to perceive what He is doing. They have eyes that would not see and ears that would not hear. This lack of spiritual perception continues to this very day."

⁹In the "Writings" section of the Old Covenant, in Psalm 69, David speaks about people's hearts being hardened against God when he says: "May their table, which is full of plenty, become a snare and a trap that makes them think all is well. May it be the stumbling block that makes them fall into the pit of retribution and punishment they

deserve. [10]May their eyes be spiritually darkened so that they cannot see. May their lives be broken continually by their lack of a spiritual backbone to uphold them when troubling times come."

4.5 Even though the Gentiles make up the majority of God's people in the present, just imagine what an amazing future is available to the people of Old Covenant Israel if they turn to Christ (11:11-32).

4.5.1 God is accomplishing a larger purpose through Old Covenant Israel's rejection (11:11-16).

[11]So, it is clear that the majority of the Jewish people missed out on receiving the Christ that God had been preparing them to receive. But have they stumbled so far away from God that they have fallen into ultimate spiritual ruin and are beyond recovery? No way! Not by any means! Rather, it is because they failed to obey God and place their faith in Christ that salvation has come to the Gentiles. In the grand scope of God's work, God now uses the salvation of the Gentiles to arouse an envy and jealousy among the Jewish people. They are jealous that the Gentiles are now considered part of God's family, and God uses this envy to entice and draw the Jewish people out of their spiritual ruin. So, no, the Jewish people have not fallen beyond spiritual recovery. God is still working to call them to faith in Christ.

[12]Just think about it: If the nation of Israel's spiritual misstep means spiritual riches for the world, and their loss means spiritual wealth for the Gentiles, how much greater riches and wealth will be brought by the Jewish peoples' full restoration into God's family through faith in Christ!

[13]Now, you Gentiles, who are a majority in God's Church, need to pay special attention to these things. You Gentiles are part of the genuine remnant of God's people, those who are the true Israel and people of God through faith in Christ. Since you are now a majority in God's Church, these words are important to help you realize that God has not abandoned the people of Israel whom He worked through during

the times of the Old Covenant. God is still at work among them to call them to faith in Christ. Make no mistake, God has appointed me as an apostle—a divinely assigned messenger—to bring His message to the Gentiles. I work hard to share God's message with the Gentiles. [14]I do so in the hope that I may somehow make the people of Israel jealous because of so many Gentiles putting their faith in God. I hope that my hard labors in the ministry will magnify God's unmerited favor, make my fellow Jewish people envious of the Gentiles who are receiving His grace, and, as a result, perhaps lead some of them to faith in Christ. [15]For if the people of Israel's rejection of Christ was the means that helped cause the spread of God's offer of salvation to the rest of the world, then can you imagine how incredible the people of Israel's acceptance of Christ will be? It will be so amazing; it will be like new life coming to those who are dead!

[16]Just think about what an incredible future Israel could have! For example, if the first portion of the dough (meaning Abraham and the other patriarchs of Israel) offered is holy and set apart for God, then it is logical to assume that the entire batch of dough (implying the people of Israel after Abraham) will be holy too. Likewise, let us use the image of the olive tree, which is an important symbolic reference to Israel, to examine this even further. If the root of the tree (meaning Abraham) is holy, then it is logical to assume that the branches (referring to the people of Israel after Abraham) will be too. Yes, what an incredible future Israel will have if their faith dynamic changes and they turn from rejecting Christ to accepting Him!

4.5.2 The pride of the New Covenant Gentiles could cause them to become lifeless, spiritual deadwood (11:17-24).

[17]However, while there are tremendous possibilities for Israel's future, the present situation is a different reality. On one hand, some of the original branches (referring to some of the people of Israel after Abraham) have been broken off from the original olive tree (meaning from God's family). On the other hand, many of you Gentiles—who were branches from a different, wild olive tree—have been grafted into the original olive tree! You now share in the nourishing sap that

comes from God's olive tree (symbolizing that you now share in the blessings promised to Abraham and his descendants).

[18]But do you realize that your being grafted into God's olive tree is an act of His grace and unmerited favor? You being grafted into God's olive tree does not make you better or superior to any other branch on God's olive tree. You have nothing to brag or be overly proud about; every branch is alike—attached by God's grace. If you are prone to think your branch is better than others, then you are missing the faith dynamic at work in God's family. You should remember this fact: You do not support the root. You are just a branch, and the root supports you!

[19]I can almost hear some overly selfish and prideful person say, "Those branches were broken off to make room for me to be grafted in." [20]Yes, them being broken off made it possible. But do not forget that these branches were broken off because of their unbelief, which caused them to become lifeless—spiritual deadwood that needed to be cut off. Remember that you are only grafted into God's olive tree and established as God's people through faith in Christ, through faith in what He has done for you. So, do not be arrogant and think your acceptance before God is because of who you are or anything you have done; it is all by God's grace! Be humbly aware of that reality and fear that if you become spiritually lifeless, like spiritual deadwood, God could cut you off too. [21]For if God did not spare the natural branches that had become lifeless from being cut off from His tree, then neither will He spare you.

[22]Be sure you do not fail to notice both the tremendous kindness and ruthless sternness of God. On one hand, He is ruthlessly stern and firm toward those who have fallen away from Him, those who have not placed their faith in Christ. On the other hand, God is tremendously kind to you, if you continue to live in His grace and kindness. Otherwise, you will also become lifeless, spiritual deadwood that will be cut off.

[23]Even though you are prone to feel spiritually superior to those people of Israel who failed to recognize Christ when He came, are you

considering how they could yet turn back to God in faith? If they do not continue in their unbelief, they will be grafted in (just as you have been), for God has the power to graft them into His olive tree again.

²⁴Think about it. You were cut out of a wild, non-native olive tree that was different from God's original olive tree (meaning the family line of God). Even though it was seemingly contrary to natural processes, God has grafted you into His cultivated olive tree, into the people who belong to Him. If He can do that with the wild, non-native branches, then how much more easily and readily can the original branches that have been cut off be grafted right back into the olive tree where they were belong?

> 4.5.3 In God's sight, there is no difference between Jew or Gentile. All must come to Him the same way—through faith in Christ (11:25-32).

²⁵My dear brothers and sisters, I do not want you to misunderstand God's mystery, to be ignorant of what was hidden in the past and miss what is now made known through the gospel. Your understanding of this theological point has practical implications. If you do not understand what God has made known, then you might become arrogant and conceited. So, let us review God's mystery, what His gospel has now made known: The people of the nation of Israel have experienced a partial hardening of their hearts. However, it is not permanent. It will only last until the full number of the Gentiles has come into God's family through faith in Christ.

²⁶Having seen the Gentiles come into God's family by turning to faith in Christ, a portion of people that is representative of all people from the nation of Israel will be saved. The Scriptures of the Old Covenant confirm that will happen. As it is written in Isaiah 59:20-21: "The Deliverer sent from God to bring salvation will come from the new, heavenly Jerusalem established after the last day, and He will turn all godlessness away from the true Israel—away from the people who belong to God." ²⁷Also, as it is written in Isaiah 27:9, "This is My covenant—My lasting commitment—with My people, when I shall take away their sins."

[28]As far as the gospel is concerned, many people of the nation of Israel are now enemies of God; they are enemies of His good news message about Christ—the good news that is for your spiritual advantage and benefit. However, because of God's sovereign choice, the people of Old Covenant Israel are still dearly loved by Him. For God chose to work through the Old Covenant Israelite patriarchs (Abraham, Isaac, Jacob, and Joseph) to prepare the way for Christ. [29]And God keeps His promises. God's gifts and His call are irrevocable; they can never be withdrawn from those who have received them.

[30]Now realize and accept this fact: There is no difference between Jew and Gentile in God's sight. At one time, you were all disobedient to God. Yet you have now received God's mercy as a result of the people of Old Covenant Israel's disobedience. [31]Likewise, they, too, have become disobedient to God in order that they may now receive God's mercy. [32]And here is the main point: Whether Jew or Gentile, we all have been made equal before God. He has made all people prisoners of disobedience, so that He might also show His great mercy to everyone equally!

4.6 Praise God for how He has been working in the past, present, and future to make His salvation available to everyone (11:33-36)!

[33]In light of everything that has been said about God's extraordinary plan for the world (which includes everyone), are you not in utter and complete awe and amazement? Just in case we need to be reminded, think about how tremendously great these three things are:

1) The depths and riches of God's kindness, wisdom, and knowledge!
2) How impossible it is for our finite minds to fully understand His divine executive decision to offer salvation to us through Christ!
3) How far beyond what our finite minds can plan are God's divine executive decisions and actions!

We can only stand in awe of God's greatness and His extraordinary plan for the world!

[34]And if that is not enough, if we need to be reminded of how far above us are God's thoughts and ways, then consider these three questions:

1) As it asks in Isaiah 40:13, "Who would be so arrogant to think they can fully know or explain the mind of the Lord?"
2) As it also asks in Isaiah 40:13, "Who would be so arrogant to think they are wise enough to tell God what He needs to do?"
3) [35]As it asks in Job 41:3, "Who is small minded enough to think he or she has given God so much that they think He owes them a debt or a favor?"

[36]So, here we are, standing in complete awe of God's extraordinary plan of salvation for the world! Everything comes from Him, exists through Him, and is intended for Him. May God's all-surpassing and great worth be recognized forever!

5. As a result of being brought into a right relationship with God through faith in Christ, God's people experience transformed relationships and transformed perspectives in every aspect of life (12:1–15:13).

   5.1 God's people experience a transformed relationship with God by continually consecrating their bodies to Him and by renewing their minds through His truth (12:1-2).

CHAPTER 12

[1]Up to this point, I have written about better understanding what we believe. In particular, we have focused on how God puts us, no matter who we are, into a right relationship with Him only by His grace through faith. However, our beliefs about God should never be separated from how we live before God. So, in light of a better

understanding of our beliefs about God, I want to shift gears now and focus on how what we believe practically transforms how we live.

With eyes wide open to a better understanding of our beliefs, my dear brothers and sisters in Christ, I beg, urge, and earnestly plead with you to live a life consistent with the gospel. When it comes to the religious life, we often focus on externals, as though our beliefs are disconnected from our bodies. We are accustomed to offering some external animal sacrifice, doing some religious ritual, or thinking of our spiritual lives as completely separate from the rest of our physical existence. But, with a consistent focus and constant dependence on God's mercies, I urge you to offer your bodies to God as a living and holy sacrifice. What does that mean? Let me explain:

- Offer *your bodies*, because a life with God includes every aspect of your being, not just the so-called spiritual aspects.
- Offer your bodies *as holy*, because your entire life, including your physical body, should be oriented toward and set apart for serving Him.
- Offer them as *living sacrifices*, because life with God is not a dead ritual but a vibrant, living relationship with Him.

Offering your bodies to God as a living and holy sacrifice is the kind of worship that is pleasing to Him. After all, this kind of reasonable worship from an informed understanding is how we should be living for God.

²In order to live this way, do not be conformed to the pattern of this world, copying its behaviors and customs. Instead, be transformed into this life with God through the renewing of your mind. As your mind is renewed into His truth, you will learn to know God's will for your life—His good, pleasing, and perfect will—which will lead you to have the life you are meant to live.

5.2 God's people experience a transformed relationship within themselves when they realize they are all part of the same body of Christ with other believers (12:3-8).

³Because of the role that God, in His grace, has called me to fulfill, I call on everyone to live out these words of instruction: Do not think more highly of yourselves than you should. Instead, use an accurate and sound judgment to think about (and realize) who you are in Christ. Measure your life by your dependence on God's grace through the faith He has given to you.

⁴While we believers are a diverse people, our common faith in Christ forms us into a unified group. Think of it like this: Just as our bodies have many parts, and each of those parts serves a different function, ⁵so it is with the people of faith who make up the body of Christ. Through our faith in Christ, we are the many varied and different parts that compose His one body. And we all belong to that same marvelous body—the body of Christ!

⁶Though we are of the same body, God has not designed us all to have the same abilities and functions. By God's free design, He has graciously given us each different gifts and abilities. And we are to put this body into action and to keep it functioning well. So, if your gift is prophesying (being able to discern the truth about a present of future circumstance), then share your insights with others in a faithful, Christ-like manner. ⁷If your gift is serving others (a special talent for serving that is beyond the normal disposition to serve that we all share), then use it to serve others well, as it will inspire others to fulfill their call to serve. If your gift is teaching, then teach and guide the community of faith into truth. ⁸If your gift is being able to encourage others, then use it to give people the encouragement they need to live for God. If your gift is being able to give to others, then give with a single-minded, generous attitude that has no ulterior motive. If your gift is leading and managing others, then work hard at it and take the responsibility seriously. If your gift is being able to recognize the needs of others and to show kindness to them, then do so with joyful eagerness.

5.3 God's people experience a transformed relationship with one another by loving others as if they are family (12:9-16).

⁹No matter what our God-given gifts and abilities are or what we think about ourselves, there is one characteristic that must pervade our lives with others. That one characteristic is this: Our love must not be hypocritical but genuine and sincere. Love that is sincere—the kind that should be demonstrated by those in God's family—will embody various characteristics. It will hate what is evil, and it will hold on to what is good. ¹⁰Love that is sincere will create a deep devotion among one another, as though the other person is a close, cherished family member. It will delight in honoring one another (like respect among beloved family members) and put the needs of others above our own. ¹¹It will never be lazy toward living a life of informed worship, but it will burn with spiritual passion in serving the Lord. ¹²Such love will persevere in worship by rejoicing in confident hope regardless of the circumstances, by being patient when faced with suffering, and by persisting in prayer. ¹³It will share with God's people when they are in need, and it will always be eager to pursue and practice hospitality toward others as people travel through life.

¹⁴Our genuine, sincere love must not be limited to those in God's family. It must be shown to everyone, even those who are not believers. Thus, you are to ask God to show divine favor on those who persecute you. Likewise, do not curse those who curse you but speak well of them. ¹⁵Care for others to such a degree that when they rejoice, you rejoice. Have so much empathy and concern for others that when they weep, you weep. ¹⁶Live in harmony with one another. Do not be so proud and full of yourself that you are not willing to associate with people of lower social standing—the down and outers, or the people working hard doing the lowly things you might be too proud to do. Never overestimate yourself; never be conceited and view yourself as too good for others; and never be wise in your own sight.

5.4 God's people experience a transformed relationship with their enemies not by retaliating against them but by serving them with sincere love (12:17-21).

[17]Our genuine and sincere love must not be limited to just those in God's family or to the ordinary, everyday people we encounter. It must also be shown to our enemies. So, do not repay anyone's evil act against you with your own evil act against them. Instead, live in such a way that others know you are honorable and always do what is right. [18]As much as it is possible—and to the degree that God's will allows you—do everything that you can to live at peace with everyone.

[19]My dear friends, do not take revenge on others. Instead, leave room for God and His wrath to address them. We can rest assured that God will not let evil go unpunished. As the Lord says in Deuteronomy 32:35: "It is My place to avenge evil; I will repay to them what they deserve." [20]Instead, we should look for ways to serve our enemies. As it says in Proverbs 25:21-22: "If your enemy is hungry, feed him; if he is thirsty, give him something to drink. In serving him like this, it will be like you are putting hot, burning coals on their heads in the hope that they will become ashamed of their actions and seek to understand the reason why you can respond with such love." [21]Be filled with genuine and sincere love, and do not be overcome by evil. Do not let it defeat you. Instead, overcome evil and defeat it by doing good.

5.5 God's people experience a transformed relationship with governing authorities in society by submitting to and respecting their authority (13:1-7).

CHAPTER 13

[1]Beyond our own relationship with the Lord and our call to sincerely love others—even our enemies—we must also recognize our broader societal responsibilities to our governing authorities. Everyone must recognize their authority in our lives and submit to them. Why? Because all authority comes from God, and the governing authorities that exist have been established and placed there by God.

²Therefore, anyone who resists the civic or governing authorities is resisting what God has instituted; they are rebelling against the authorities God has put in place. Whoever rebels against governing authorities is reflecting a spiritual state of rebellion—the type that may receive civic punishment now, but more importantly the type of rebelliousness God will eradicate and punish at the end of human history.

³One of the purposes of government is that it serves God now by rewarding good and punishing evil. The governing authorities do not strike fear in people who are doing right, but they do strike fear in those who are doing wrong. Do you want to live without any fear of the civic or governing authorities? Then do what is right, and they will commend you for it. ⁴Those in government and civic positions of authority are God's servants; they have been placed there by God for your good. But if you are someone who does wrong, then it is only natural that you should be afraid of them. For God does not allow them to bear the sword—to have the power to punish—for no reason. Right now, they are serving God by acting as an extension of His wrath and His punishment against evil in this world, and by bringing punishment upon those who do wrong.

⁵Therefore, you must submit to your governing authorities. You should submit to them not just to avoid punishment but also as a means of maintaining a clear conscience, knowing that you are living and doing as God desires. ⁶As such, fulfill your obligations as citizens within your government structures. Your life of faith in Christ should not be disconnected from fulfilling your duties to the societal structures and governmental authorities God has put in place. So be a good citizen and pay your taxes, for the civic authorities are serving God's purposes in what they do, devoting their time and effort to governing. ⁷Give to everyone what you owe them. If there are taxes to be paid, pay them. If there are other government fees that are collected, pay them. If a person is in a governmental position of authority, respect it and honor their position of authority.

5.6 God's people experience a transformed relationship toward God's moral law by embodying the love of Christ, which fulfills the Law (13:8-10).

[8]You should always pay your bills and take care of your financial obligations. However, in God's economy, there is only one debt that can never be paid back completely: that is your debt to love other people. You should be paying back this debt of love every day. Yet you should realize that, as a follower of Christ, you have a debt that you will spend your entire life attempting to pay off yet can never fulfill.

Here is the tremendous reality about love and how God would have us to live: If you love one another genuinely and sincerely, then you have fulfilled God's moral law and fulfilled His desire for how He would have you live in the world. [9]You can see this by looking at what a few of the Old Covenant commandments say: "You shall not commit adultery. You shall not murder. You shall not steal. You shall not desire to possess what belongs to someone else." Each of these Old Covenant commandments and words of instruction on how to live— and the other commandments in the remainder of the Old Covenant scriptures—are summed up in the one New Covenant command from Jesus: "Love your neighbor as you love yourself." [10]Love that is genuine and sincere, the kind of love you should have, does no harm or wrong to others. Therefore, when we love others like this, as Christ would, it fulfills the requirements of the Old Covenant commandments and embodies the kind of life God wants us to live now.

5.7 God's people experience a transformed relationship toward the end of time by realizing that God is working in His people now to develop in them the fullness of life that is yet to come (13:11-14).

[11]Given that we are living in this critically important time, the time right before Christ's return and His second coming, we understand the urgency to embody God's love and do all the things we have talked about: to think about ourselves humbly, to use our God-given gifts and abilities to serve others, to love genuinely and sincerely, to submit

to the authority of government and those in positions of authority, and to live a life of love that fulfills God's desire for our lives. Yes, the appointed hour has come for you to wake up from your lazy and sleepy slumber. It is time for you to embody God's truth, love others in a Christ-like manner, and put these things into practice. For our final salvation in God's plan is nearer to us now than when we first believed.

[12]The night darkened by sin's stain is almost over; the new day of God's ultimate salvation will soon be here. So then, let us take off our dirty clothes stained by our dark and sinful deeds. Let us put on the shining armor of God's light, which enables us to be victorious in our spiritual battle. [13]Since we now live in this new day and new life, let us walk through our daily lives reflecting God's light. Let us avoid the behaviors associated with spiritual darkness, things such as participating in orgies, drinking to drunkenness, engaging in sexual promiscuity and immoral living, fostering dissension or bickering, and fostering jealousy. [14]Instead, clothe yourselves with the Lord Jesus Christ, and do not let yourselves think about ways to gratify the desires of your sinful, human nature.

5.8 God's people experience a transformed relationship toward those who have different religious perspectives and practices by realizing that what unites them as part of God's family is stronger and more important than their differences (14:1–15:13).

5.8.1 *Do not condemn and pass judgment on fellow members in your family of faith (14:1-12).*

CHAPTER 14

[1]As followers of Christ, the gospel transforms our attitudes toward one another. As God transforms us, we discover that our unity in Christ is more important than our individual perspectives and opinions on non-essential religious matters. For example, there are those among you who are labeled "weak" and those labeled "strong" because of

differences in their religious practices. Those labeled "weak" are Jewish followers of Christ who like to continue practicing the Old Covenant [Old Testament] traditions they have observed all their lives. They continue these traditions as spiritual practices that help them connect with God. They are not living according to the Old Covenant by trusting in these acts to supplant or replace their dependence on God's grace through faith in Christ. They have accepted God's New Covenant through Christ. Yet, because they continue these spiritual practices as a means of relating to God, they are considered "weak" by the Gentile followers of Christ who make up the majority among you.

Then there are those labeled "strong" among you, followers of Christ who feel no need to observe or practice these spiritual traditions or rituals from the Old Covenant.

But no matter which side of the issue you are on, let me be crystal clear about how your attitude and treatment of one another should be. In short, you need to stop judging each other! Your genuine attitude should be not only to receive the "weak" one you disagree with but to realize that you have such a deep, common bond with them that you treat them like they are vital part of your dearly loved family. Your common bond with them should be so strong that you readily accept them—with no hesitation—into your home, your circle of friends, your social groups, and among all those who think as you do.

And just so we are clear: Your attitude and deep, common bond with your fellow believers should be so strong that when you accept them, the genuine love and unity you share should so dominate your minds that arguing with them about who is right and wrong does not even enter your thoughts.

²You see, genuine followers of Christ can have differences of opinion. One person's conviction about their faith will allow them to eat anything they want. Yet the so-called "weak" person's conviction about their faith will only allow them to be a vegetarian. ³But while opinions and perspectives can differ, it is up to both sides to have the proper attitude toward one another. Those whose convictions allow them to freely eat anything must not look down on (or inwardly reject) those

whose faith convictions do not allow them to freely eat whatever they want. Likewise, those whose convictions do not allow them to eat certain foods must not judge or condemn those whose faith convictions allow them to freely eat whatever food they desire. Why? Because God has accepted them into His family. [4]After all, who do you think you are to judge and condemn the faith convictions of Someone else's servant? Their own Master will judge them, deciding whether they will stand in the Lord's favor or fall out of it. With the Lord's enabling help and grace, those whose faith convictions in Christ are different than yours will stand and receive His approval the same as everyone else.

[5]And differences of opinion are not limited to religious observances related to food. Some consider one day as more sacred than another (and like to observe certain "holy days"). Yet others consider every day just as sacred as the next. What matters in these differences? Only that each person is fully convinced in their own mind of their religious acts and spiritual practices of devotion.

[6]What matters above all else is that any religious act or spiritual practice is done to honor the Lord. Those who consider certain days as special or those who set aside certain "holy days" to worship, they do so to honor the Lord. Those who feel free to eat any kind of food, they do so to honor the Lord, for they give thanks to God before eating. And those who choose not to eat certain foods, they also do so to honor the Lord, for they give thanks to God as well.

[7]We must not forget that none of us live for ourselves alone, and none of us die for ourselves alone. [8]As a follower of Christ, if we live, we live for the Lord. If we die, we die for the Lord. So, whether we live or die, either way, we belong to the Lord.

[9]And do you realize that it is for this very reason that Christ died and returned to life—that He might be the Lord of both the dead and the living? Likewise, do you realize that since He is the Lord and rules over the entire spectrum of existence, we are free from needing to judge others? He is more than capable of just judgment and does not need our help. [10]So then, why do you judge the faith convictions of your brothers and sisters in Christ? Why do you look down on

them and condemn their faith? When you find yourself starting to judge others, you would do well to remember that it is God who is the Judge and the One who judges, and that we will all stand before His judgment seat.

[11]Scripture tells us very plainly that we will all stand before God. It is written in Isaiah 45:23: "'As surely as I am the living God', says the Lord, 'every knee will bow before Me, and every tongue will confess to God.'" [12]So, do not forget that each and every one of us will have to stand before His pure, holy, and completely accurate judgment and give a full account of our lives to God.

5.8.2 Do not act in such a way that will cause your brother or sisters in Christ to stumble spiritually (14:13-23).

[13]In light of the sobering reality that we will all stand before God's judgment, let us stop passing judgment on one another. Instead, let us make up our minds to live in such a way that our lives do not become a spiritual stumbling block (or an obstacle causing the spiritual downfall) for our brothers and sisters in Christ. [14]I know and am convinced in the Lord Jesus that nothing is unclean (that we are not spiritually defiled by touching certain things in the everyday world). However, if someone's beliefs convict them that certain things are unclean, then for that person it is unclean (and would be wrong to touch). And you should respect that. [15]Moreover, if your brother or sister in Christ is distressed by your freedom to eat certain things, then are you acting in love toward them if you eat it? Do not let your spiritual freedom to eat anything you want be the means of driving someone away from the faith and causing their ultimate spiritual ruin. After all, that person is someone for whom Christ died. [16]If you live with this kind of gracious consideration and thoughtfulness for the spiritual well-being of others, then no one will speak evil of the good thing you enjoy, or of the spiritual freedom you enjoy through faith in Christ.

[17]Remember: The values of the kingdom of God are bigger and more important than our differences. For the kingdom of God is not a matter of what we eat or what we drink, but of embodying a life of ethical behavior that reflects Christ, living in peaceful harmony with one

another, and experiencing a life of joy in the Holy Spirit. [18]Whoever serves Christ in this way—living a life guided by the values of the kingdom of God—is pleasing to God, and they will be approved by others as well.

[19]Since we are called to live these kingdom values, let us make every effort to do what leads to peaceful harmony with one another. Let us actively engage each other in the act of building up and strengthening each other's faith. [20]Do not tear apart God's work over differences of opinion on religious practices, such as what is okay to eat. You who are in the majority are right in that all food is clean and does not cause spiritual harm. However, it is wrong for you to abuse your spiritual freedom to eat anything you want if you know that eating it can cause another person to lose their spiritual balance. [21]It is much better to use your spiritual freedom to abstain from eating meat, drinking wine, or doing anything that will cause another believer to stumble into a spiritual downfall.

[22]So, whatever your personal faith convictions are on differing religious practices and perspectives, keep them between yourself and God. After all, any opinion on religious matters can be wrong if it does not come from faith and embody kingdom values. For example, on the positive side, those who have not condemned themselves by abusing their spiritual freedom to cause the spiritual downfall of others have a divine sense of fulfillment and satisfaction. [23]However, on the negative side, if you have doubts about whether something is religiously acceptable—such as eating certain kinds of food—and if you eat it anyway, then you are causing your own spiritual downfall because you are not being true to your convictions and are not acting from faith. Every action that does not come from faith—everything done without a conviction of its approval by God—is sinful and misses the mark of what God desires for our lives.

5.8.3 *Follow the example of Christ and put other people first*
(15:1-6).

CHAPTER 15

¹Instead, those of us who are "strong" in our faith convictions should
so identify with the so-called "weak" who do not share our views
about certain freedoms that their burdens and concerns become our
burdens and concerns. We should help them to carry their burdens
and strive to relieve their concerns. We should not live to please ourselves. ²Each one of us should make it a habitual practice to put other
people first. We should be interested in what is good for the people
around us and what serves their spiritual well-being. Each one of us
should act in ways that build others up into what is for their good and
spiritual benefit. ³We follow Christ's example, for He did not live to
please Himself. Instead, Christ gave no thought to Himself and served
us through His suffering. As it is written in Psalm 69:9: "The insults
of those who insult you have fallen on Me, and I now carry them."

⁴Remember, all of the scriptures written in the past were written to
teach us. When we read about the patient endurance of the faithful
ones and the help God gave them, we receive encouragement from
the scriptures. And this encouragement from the scriptures provides
us with the spiritual nourishment we need to hold on strongly to the
ultimate hope of our salvation.

⁵As you follow the example of Christ Jesus, may the God who gives
patient endurance and encouragement enable each one of you to have
the same humble attitude of mind toward one another. May you be
of one mind, having the attitude of Christ Jesus in you, so that you
may live in complete harmony with one another. ⁶Then you all will
be thinking as though you have one mind and speaking as though
you have one voice. And from this one mind and one voice, together,
you will acknowledge and praise the all-surpassing value and worth of
God, the Father of our Lord Jesus Christ.

5.8.4 Christ fulfilling God's promise brings God's divine favor to all who have faith. As a result, treat each person of faith as though they are dearly loved family members who belong to God (15:7-13).

⁷As we come toward the end of this letter, let me remind you of a key point I have been making throughout it: By fulfilling His Old Covenant promises of salvation through Christ, God has brought His New Covenant grace and favor to everyone—both the Jews and the Gentiles. Through faith in Christ, God is both transforming individual lives and transforming our community.

In light of this truth, even though you will have differences as believers, you are to be so accepting of one another that you welcome each other into your homes, social circles, and communities—treating each other as dearly loved family. We are to welcome each other in this way because this is how Christ has welcomed each one of us into the family of God. When we welcome each other in this manner, and when we live together in the common unity of our faith, we honor and glorifies God.

⁸Do you see the great balance among you all in what I have been saying—the balance in God's plan for both Jews and Gentiles? For Christ came as a servant to the Jews so that everyone could see and know God's truth. And Christ's life of service to the Jews served Gods' truth in two distinct ways. First, He showed the Jews that God is faithful, and that God has fulfilled His promises to the spiritual patriarchs of the Old Covenant. ⁹Second, Christ showed that the Gentiles can ascribe ultimate worth to God, for God has extended His mercy and salvation to them as well.

We can see God preparing us for this one, united community—which is forged by His grace and includes both Jew and Gentile—through every major section of the Old Covenant scriptures, which are the Law, Prophets, and Writings. In the Writings sections of the Old Covenant, in Psalm 18:49, it is written: "Because of this, I will praise you among the Gentiles; I will sing the praises of your name."

¹⁰In the "Law" section of the Old Covenant, in Deuteronomy 32:43, it highlights how the wall of hostility—which was a literal, physical wall at the Temple that separated the Jews from the outer courts of the Gentiles and signified they were outside of God's family—has been broken down; it says, "You Gentiles are able to rejoice fully together with God's people."

¹¹Again, in the "Writings" section of the Old Covenant, in Psalm 117:1, it speaks of the common unity that Jew and Gentile will share: "Praise the Lord, all you Gentiles. Praise Him, all you people of the earth."

¹²In the "Prophets" section of the Old Covenant, in Isaiah 11:10, it foretells the same salvation you both will share: "The Root of Jesse— the One who comes from the family lineage of David—will spring up, and He will rise up to rule over all the nations. The Gentiles will place their hope for salvation in Him."

¹³As I wrap up this point—that God has intended for both the Jews and the Gentiles to be formed into one body by His grace—I want to share my prayer with you. I pray that the God who is the Source and Giver of hope will fill all your lives with two kingdom values. First, I pray that you will not only experience but also be filled with joy and peace as you trust in Christ. Second, I pray that, through the power of the Holy Spirit, you will overflow with the hope of salvation you all share.

6. Conclusion: God is at work through Paul's ministry (15:14–16:27).

6.1 Paul reflects on all that Christ has done in and through him and on his future ministry plans (15:14-21).

¹⁴I hope this letter does not seem like doom and gloom. To the contrary, I am confident and fully convinced, my fellow brothers and

sisters in Christ, that you are full of moral goodness! I am writing not to a community of novices in their walk with Christ, or to a deeply sinful people. Instead, I am writing to a community of Christ-followers who are both knowledgeable about their faith and who practice it. I have heard from others that you are very knowledgeable, that you know these things so well that you could teach them to others. [15]Yet I have spoken to you quite boldly on important points in several parts of this letter. Let me explain why. First, since you are very knowledgeable of the truth, I spoke boldly to remind you of and focus your attention on the truth that you already know. Second, I spoke boldly to you because God's grace has called me, making it my ambition, [16]to be a servant of Christ Jesus to the Gentiles. God has given me this priest-like duty of proclaiming His good news of Christ. He gave me this duty so that the Gentiles, through their faith in Christ, might be an offering acceptable to God, as they are made holy through the ongoing work of the Holy Spirit.

[17]As I reflect on all that Christ Jesus has done during my service to Him, I am excited and proud of all He has done among the Gentiles. [18]And I will not be so bold to speak of any accomplishments as though they were my own. I can only speak of what Christ has done through me to accomplish His larger goal among the Gentiles: leading them to follow and obey God. God has used what I have said and done, [19]has put His power on display through miraculous signs and wonders that accompanied His Word and has used the power of the Spirit of God to lead people to follow and obey the truth.

As I reflect on what God has led me to do thus far in my service to Him, I feel that I have completed a vital phase of the work He that has called me to do. From Jerusalem to all the way around the immediate Gentile, Mediterranean world, I have presented the gospel of Christ and left behind an embedded community of believers. [20]As a result of what God has called me to do, it has always been my ambition to proclaim God's good news in places where Christ is not known rather than building upon a foundation that someone else has already started, and that is what I have been doing. [21]I have been fulfilling what God said in Isaiah 52:15, where it is written, "Those who have

never heard about Him will have their eyes opened, and those who
have never heard of Him will come to understand."

6.2 Paul shares his immediate travel plans to visit the people of Rome on his way to Spain (15:22-29).

²²If you are wondering why I have not yet come to visit you, that is
why—because I have been actively proclaiming Christ in those places
where He is not yet known. And that service has delayed me from
coming to visit you. ²³But now, I have finished my work in these
regions, and I am in a transitional phase of my ministry. After many
years of longing to visit you, I am finally able.

²⁴My plans for the near future are to go to Spain. On my journey to
Spain, I hope to stop and visit with you for a while along the way.
After I have had the pleasure of enjoying your company, I also hope
to gain your logistical support for my further missionary endeavors.
²⁵However, before I can come to you, I must first go to Jerusalem to
serve the Lord's people there. I must deliver a gift to them. ²⁶The reason: The Gentile followers of Christ in the wealthy areas of Macedonia
and Achaia were eager to make a tangible contribution to help support
the poor among the followers of Christ in Jerusalem. ²⁷The Gentile
believers were glad to provide their support and offer this gift; they
feel they owe these Jewish believers a spiritual debt. Since the Gentiles
have received the spiritual blessings of God's good news through these
Jewish believers, they feel the least they can do is share their financial
blessings with them.

²⁸As soon as I have completed this task, making sure the Jerusalem
believers understand that the Gentiles have made this loving gesture
as an expression of their love and unity in Christ with them, then I
will begin my journey toward Spain, and I will stop to visit with you
on the way. ²⁹I eagerly anticipate the time of my arrival with you in
Rome, because by that time I will have given those in Jerusalem the
Gentile's gift, and I will be able to enjoy the full measure of the spiritual encouragement, joy, and favor that Christ will give to us during
our time together.

6.3 Paul requests prayer from the Romans (15:30-33).

³⁰But as much as I anticipate the future time of my visit, my dear brothers and sisters in Christ, I have an urgent prayer request for you in the present. By the authority of and in the will of our Lord Jesus Christ, and by the love that the Holy Spirit fosters among us, I urge you to join me in the struggle of my missionary work by praying to God for me. ³¹I would like to ask you to pray for two things specifically. First, pray that I will be kept safe from unbelievers—those who disobey God—in Judea (as I have encountered issues with them in my past travels). Second, pray that the followers of Christ in Jerusalem will accept the financial gift and donation I am brining to them from the Gentiles (that they will not refuse it as coming from the hands of unholy or unclean Gentiles, which would be an unhealthy attitude that their former Old Covenant ways could lead them to have). ³²Once this work has been accomplished, by the will of God, I will be able to come to you in the fullness of joy; I look forward to being spiritually refreshed and encouraged by visiting you. ³³But until then, my prayer for you is that the God who is the source of and giver of peace may be with you all. And may it always be so.

6.4 Paul sends personal greetings to a variety of people in Rome (16:1-16).

CHAPTER 16

6.4.1 Paul commends one of his ministry colleagues (16:1-2).

¹As you know, people traveling in our society depend on the assistance of others to help meet their needs along their journey. Our fellow servants and missionaries traveling to serve Christ depend on it even more. So, let me give you an endorsement to support our sister Phoebe. She is an officially appointed leader serving the church in Cenchrea. ²I ask that you give her an enthusiastic welcome in the Lord. Welcome her as one who is worthy of honor among God's people for her dedicated service. Give her any help and support she needs

from you, for she has helped so many people with financial support, including me.

6.4.2 Paul gives his personal greetings (16:3-15).

³Also, please give my personal greetings to the following people:

Say hello for me to the husband and wife team of Priscilla and Aquila, for they have been my fellow coworkers in serving Christ Jesus. ⁴They have risked their lives for me, and I am grateful for all they have done not just for me but for all the Gentile churches as well. ⁵Also, give my greetings to the church that meets in their house.

Say hello for me to my dear friend Epenetus, who was the first convert in the province of Asia.

⁶Say hello for me to Mary, who has worked very hard for your benefit.

⁷Say hello for me to the husband and wife team of Andronicus and Junia. They are not only my relatives with Jewish backgrounds who follow Christ, but they have also been in prison with me for their witness. They are well-known and highly respected in our missionary community, and they were followers of Christ before I was.

⁸Say hello for me to Ampilatus, my good friend in the Lord.

⁹Say hello for me to Urbanus, our fellow coworker in Christ, and also my good friend Stachys.

¹⁰Say hello for me to Apelles, a man known for his faithfulness and loyalty to Christ.

Say hello for me to all the believers who are slaves belonging to the household of Aristobulus.

¹¹Say hello for me to Herodion, a fellow believer with a Jewish background.

Say hello for me to those who follow the Lord who are slaves belonging to the household of Narcissus.

¹²Say hello for me to Tryphena and Tryphosa, women who have worked hard serving the Lord.

Say hello for me to Persis, another woman who has been diligent in her work for the Lord.

¹³Say hello for me to Rufus, the one who was chosen by the Lord to carry His cross. Also, send my greetings to his mother, who has been like a mother to me as well.

¹⁴Say hello for me to Asyncritus, Phlegon, Hermes, Patrobas, Hermas, and the other brothers and sisters in Christ who live in community with them.

¹⁵Say hello for me to Philologus, Julia, Nereus and his sister, and to Olympas and all the believers who live in community with them.

6.4.3 Paul encourages the Romans to welcome each other and sends greetings from other churches (16:16).

¹⁶As in customary in our culture, be kind and welcome each other with a holy kiss.

Also, know that all the churches of Christ send their greetings and well wishes to you, the church in Rome.

6.5 Paul shares a final message and praises God for His plan of salvation through Christ (16:17-27).

6.5.1 Paul's warning: Avoid divisive persons (16:17-20).

PAUL GIVES A FINAL WARNING

¹⁷Before finishing this letter, let me leave one final word of urgent guidance with you. My dear brothers and sisters in Christ, I urge you

to watch out for those who create divisions and cause spiritual obstacles that are contrary to the teaching that you have learned. Stay away
from them; avoid them. [18]People that fall into these two categories—
creating divisions or causing spiritual obstacles for others—are not
serving our Lord Christ. Instead, they are serving their own appetites,
interests, and preferred way of living. You must be alert and on the
lookout for them, because they are very effective and persuasive talk-
ers. Through their smooth talk and flattery, they are able to deceive
many innocent, sincere people. [19]Thankfully, you have earned a solid
reputation for your faithful obedience to the Lord. This causes me
great joy! But I could not end this letter without sharing this urgent
guidance with you, because I want you to be wise and well versed in
doing good and what is right, and to be innocent of evil and what is
wrong.

**PAUL REMINDS THE ROMANS TO FOCUS ON GOD'S FUTURE GLORY AND
GIVES A FINAL PRAYER FOR DIVINE FAVOR (16:20).**

[20]And let us not lose sight of the day that is coming soon—that great
day when the God of peace will crush Satan under your feet.

Until then, may the grace and supernatural favor of our Lord Jesus
Christ be with you.

6.5.2 Paul's friends send their greetings (16:21-24).

[21]Also, several people who are here with me wanted to send their greetings and say hello to you. Timothy, my fellow coworker, says hello
to you. So does Lucius, Jason, and Sosipater, for they are my fellow
followers of Christ who come from a Jewish background. [22]I, Tertius,
have been the one acting as Paul's amanuensis—serving as his trained
scribe writing down what Paul has dictated—for this letter. I also send
my personal greeting to you as one who is in the Lord. [23]Gaius, whose
hospitality I and the whole church here enjoy, says hello. Erastus, the
city's director of public works, sends his greeting, as does our brother
Quartus. [Some manuscripts include: "[24]May the grace of our Lord
Jesus Christ be with you all, and may be it always be so."]

6.5.3 Praise God for His salvation through Christ (16:25-27).

[25]Now, as we conclude this letter, let us draw our attention to where it should be: recognizing the all-surpassing value and worth of God and giving all our glory to Him. Let us give glory to the One who calls you to salvation—the One who is able to establish and strengthen you into a transformed life through His good news about Christ, which I have been communicating with you. This message about Jesus Christ is the good news of salvation for all people that God has now fully revealed and made known. For many long ages in the past, the full revelation of God's plan was not fully known. It was almost like a hidden secret. [26]But now, as the prophets of the Old Covenant foretold and as our eternal God has commanded, God's full plan for salvation has been revealed. It has been made known to all the Gentiles everywhere, so that they too might come to the Spirit-empowered, obedient lifestyle that comes through faith in the Lord. [27]May the only wise God, the One who has implemented such a wonderful plan of salvation, be esteemed as the most valuable treasure forever through Jesus Christ! May it always be so.

CPSIA information can be obtained
at www.ICGtesting.com
Printed in the USA
BVHW060322230120
570202BV00006B/556